Sister Benedicta Ward read history at t[...] theology at Oxford. A supernumera[...] College, she teaches church history and spirituality for the Faculty of Theology at the University of Oxford and is the Reader in the History of Christian Spirituality, specializing in early Church and medieval spirituality. Sister Benedicta is a member of the Anglican religious community of the Sisters of the Love of God, and has written a number of books on early monasticism and aspects of the Middle Ages.

Ralph Waller is the Principal of Harris Manchester College, and Director of the Farmington Institute. He is an authority on the Wesleys and Nonconformist spirituality.

Joy of Heaven

Springs of Christian Spirituality

Edited by

BENEDICTA WARD

AND

RALPH WALLER

First published in Great Britain in 2003 by
Society for Promoting Christian Knowledge
Holy Trinity Church
Marylebone Road
London NW1 4DU

British Library Cataloguing-in-Publication Data
A catalogue record for this book is available from the British Library

ISBN 0-281-05496-7

1 3 5 7 9 10 8 6 4 2

Typeset by Kenneth Burnley, Wirral, Cheshire
Printed in Great Britain by
The Cromwell Press, Trowbridge, Wiltshire

CONTENTS

List of contributors vii

Foreword ix
Archbishop Rowan Williams

1 The Beginnings of the Jesus Prayer 1
Kallistos Ware

2 The Our Father 30
Benedicta Ward

3 On Praying the Apostles' Creed 56
David Moss

4 Hail Mary 75
Santha Bhattacharji

5 The Beatitudes 88
Jeremy Sheehy

6 Psalm 23 103
Gordon Mursell

7 Hymns of Charles Wesley 109
Ralph Waller

8 The Battle Hymn of the Republic 121
J. R. Watson

Index 143

CONTRIBUTORS

Santha Bhattacharji teaches Old and Middle English at New College, Oxford. She has a special interest in women's writing and medieval mystics.

David Moss is Director of Adult Education in the diocese of Exeter and formerly Vice-Principal of St Stephen's House, Oxford. He has written on the theme of friendship and specializes in systematic theology.

Gordon Mursell is Dean of Birmingham Cathedral and the author of *English Spirituality* (SPCK, 2001).

Jeremy Sheehy is Principal of St Stephen's House, Oxford.

Kallistos Ware is Orthodox Bishop of Diokleia and formerly Fellow of Pembroke College, Oxford. He is the author of *The Orthodox Way* and an authority on Orthodox spirituality.

J. R. Watson is Emeritus Professor of English Literature at the University of Durham.

Rowan Williams is the Archbishop of Canterbury and a published author.

FOREWORD

Writing about 'spirituality' is an odd enterprise; it is tempting to say that, just as the poetry is what gets lost in translation, so the spirituality is what gets lost in the writing. Literature about the spiritual life may look like an attempt to pin down what resists being pinned down. In an age when we have become familiar with the idea that people can describe themselves as 'spiritual but not religious', when the spiritual has come to signify precisely the opposite of dogmatic religion, there is bound to be some suspicion of writing that has its roots firmly within a doctrinally committed community. At best, spiritual writing could only be a loose and evocative, inspirational style; you may or may not get the point – as with poetry, once again.

If you turn to St John of the Cross, John Wesley, Gregory the Great or even Julian of Norwich with this conception of the spiritual in mind, you may be disappointed. Much of the litera-ture discussed in this volume engages in what can be quite a tough analysis of ideas; most of it presupposes a normative pattern of Christian teaching in the background, and the practices of a disciplined community. Even when it involves evocative and imaginative language, this is permeated by the language of a tradition, a shared story. To read such material sympathetically, you need to grasp that the point of this kind of writing is not quite the point that a modern writer of 'inspira-tional' literature might have in mind. The goal is something that will make a difference to a community of people regularly using a *canon* – not only a Bible, but a set of familiar and authoritative metaphors – and sharing definitive actions.

What kind of a difference? The difference made by the testimony that the fundamental stories and practices affect particular lives; that they have in them a continuing potential for extending the range of meaning experienced in a human life. Doctrine, left to itself, may be seen as the description of states of affairs that are simply 'out there'; the literature this book deals with not only tells us that doctrinal language is the map of a territory to be explored, it also offers the records of specific explorations. The sheer variety of records becomes itself a doctrinal datum of a sort: what manner of story is this that even such very different personal histories can reflect it and open it up further?

Sometimes this is achieved rather paradoxically by that strand in the literature that appears to dissolve or deconstruct the language of doctrine. The point comes where definitions and formulae seem like empty noises, or simply look irrelevant. But this is not a point where tradition gives way to the modern style of spiritual witness, replacing doctrinal faith with personal sensibility. It is rather that the words have become too close, too large to be seen clearly; or that the scope and depth of meaning that are being laid bare are so much more than an initial understanding might suggest that the words appear inadequate (as of course they are) to carry the reality. In either case, what is happening is a process in which what was familiar becomes strange: not false, not superseded, but problematic or alien-ating. To find out the sense in which the words are true will require time and suffering and hope.

So the words of this literature will often have the task of slowing us down in our religious talking. They may do this by the extravagance of their imagery – the complex parable, the erotic metaphor; or by their spare and restrained character. Sometimes they do it by – you could almost say – frightening us out of ordinary sense, letting us know how useless is a great part of what we try to say about God. This is not writing that is meant to make things easy; not because it puts difficult ideas before us, but because it requires of us a difficult shift in the way we see ourselves and our own experience. It requires us to find ourselves within the patterns of the great Christian story of the threefold God who makes human beings to reflect the divine beauty and identifies with the unbeautifulness of our condition in the crucified Jesus so as to restore us to where we should be, in his intimate presence. It tells us that God's action is a sort of eternal losing and finding, or leaving and homecoming; and if that is the reality at the base of our reality and all reality, we must look at our lives anew.

Who is 'spiritual literature' for? There is a problem here. One modern writer has said that a lot of this is addressed to persons who don't always yet exist: that is, it intends to speak to readers who have already begun on the road of discipline and growth; but most of us who pick up the texts are not yet there or anywhere near. That is a rather discouraging thing to think about at first sight. But it is important to remember; it means that we have to be aware that our initial responses to what we read are not necessarily going to be appropriate or 'fair'. As we read, we have to imagine what is notoriously almost impossible to imagine – a mind, a sensibility, that is greater or deeper than our own. We need help, of course, to find our way through what is simply difficult because of cultural or historical distance; but we need help also to be patient with the spiritual distance that may suddenly open up. We need to learn how to leave space for the text to be itself, and not assume that our largely secularized and self-oriented ways of contemporary reading will instantly deliver what is there to be understood.

That does not mean that such texts are beyond criticism, and that we have to dress up in period costume to read them. They are human writings, marked often by human oddities and failings. But if we simply begin by noting that this or that writer is moulded by psychological obsessions or class insensitivity or commitment to what seems an impossible theological position, we are in danger of missing what is distinctive here, which is most fundamentally the way in which each particular voice is being 'pressured' by the history of God's dealing with the world. A Christian life may be a sacrament, a statement of how God acts, even when it is involved in what we can't help seeing as error or prejudice. And this may have something rather significant to say to us in a contemporary context where it is often tempting to say that those who do not hold exactly the views we regard as correct or normative cannot be signs of Christ to us.

Disagreement does not absolve us from looking for that 'pressure' of God's action in Christ and what imprint it leaves on the lives of those who stand with us in the adventure of faith.

Reading the great texts of the Christian spiritual tradition, then, is not always a simple enterprise. We have to expect to be taken where we might not want to go, to find ourselves stranger than we thought, to try and overcome the strangeness of what we read, not only in its cultural ambience but in its inner impulses. But if we are believers, we should read in awareness of how there is a kind of 'apologetic' within the texts: the faith is that much more credible because it can take flesh in such varied ways, across so many frontiers. And if we are not believers, or not very orthodox believers, we can still allow ourselves to be introduced into a different world of self-understanding and even a different sense of how language itself works on occasion. Whatever our starting-point, the landscape after reading is different, if we can read with patience and self-questioning.

ROWAN WILLIAMS

1

THE BEGINNINGS OF
THE JESUS PRAYER

KALLISTOS WARE

Lord Jesus Christ,
Son of God,
have mercy on me.

Four intertwined threads

Without interruption, whether asleep or awake, eating,
drinking, or in company, let your heart inwardly and
mentally at times be meditating on the Psalms, at other times
be repeating the prayer 'Lord Jesus Christ, Son of God, have
mercy on me'.

Such is the brief and clear teaching on inner prayer given by
Abba Philemon, a priest-monk living in Egypt, possibly in the
sixth or early seventh century.[1] Mindful of St Paul's injunction,
'Pray without ceasing' (1 Thessalonians 5.17), Philemon wishes
our prayer to be so far as possible 'without interruption' and
continual. We are to pray, not merely during the appointed
times set apart for liturgical or private prayer, but at every
moment and in every place. Prayer is to be present in our heart
during all our daily tasks: eating, drinking, at work, not only
when in solitude but equally when in company; it is even to
extend from our waking hours into our sleep.

How, then, are we to maintain this uninterrupted remembrance of God? Philemon recommends two possibilities:
meditation on the Psalms and the frequent repetition of the
invocation 'Lord Jesus Christ, Son of God, have mercy on me'
(seven words in Greek: *Kyrie Iesou Christe, Hyie Theou, eleison me*).
This short phrase has come to be known in the Orthodox

1

Church as the Jesus Prayer, and it is a way of praying that has exercised an immense influence upon the spirituality of the Christian East – not least in our own time, when it is probably being practised more widely than ever before, by lay people as well as monastics.[2] Yet significantly Philemon mentions the Psalms alongside the invocation of the Name. The Jesus Prayer enjoys no monopoly; it is one way of attaining inner prayer – a way greatly loved by countless Christians, non-Orthodox as well as Orthodox – but it is by no means the only way.

The phrase proposed by Philemon, 'Lord Jesus Christ, Son of God, have mercy on me', constitutes what has come to be regarded as the standard or classic form of the Jesus Prayer; the *Life of Abba Philemon* is in fact the first known occasion on which this precise formula is to be found. But the Jesus Prayer can take many other forms. Two near-contemporaries of Abba Philemon, St Barsanuphius and St John of Gaza (*c.* 500–40), suggest a variety of phrases, such as 'Lord Jesus Christ, have mercy on me', 'Jesus, help me', and 'Jesus, Master, protect me'. Many people today prefer to say at the end 'have mercy on us', thus underlining our coinherence with all humankind. Another widespread variant is to conclude with the words 'have mercy on me the sinner', thereby giving to the prayer a more strongly penitential spirit.[3]

There are also numerous other mutations. Those who have been practising the Jesus Prayer for a fairly prolonged period often find that the standard form contains too many words, and they are drawn to a briefer invocation: 'Lord Jesus, have mercy', 'Lord Jesus', or else – with an intensely personal emphasis – 'My Jesus'.[4] It is also possible to say no more than the name 'Jesus' on its own; but this, though widespread in the medieval West,[5] is uncommon in Eastern Christendom. Alternatively the Prayer may be expanded. We may say 'Son of the living God' (compare Matthew 16.16), or we may incorporate the communion of saints into our invocation of the Name: 'Lord Jesus Christ, at the prayers of the Mother of God, have mercy on me', or 'at the prayers of all the saints', 'at the prayers of St *N*' (inserting one's patron saint or the saint of the day), or 'through the protection of my guardian angel'.[6]

The one unvarying component, the single root beneath the many branches, is the employment of the actual name 'Jesus'. There are other short prayers eminently suitable for frequent repetition, most notably 'Maranatha', meaning 'Our Lord, come!' or 'Our Lord has come' (see 1 Corinthians 16.22); but this cannot legitimately be called a 'Jesus Prayer' since it does not contain the name of Jesus. By contrast, the exclamation 'Come, Lord Jesus!' (Revelation 22.20) can indeed be classified as a form of the Jesus Prayer. In principle, any short formula may be seen as an expression of the Jesus Prayer, so long as it contains the specific appellation 'Jesus'.[7]

What are the origins of the Jesus Prayer, understood in this wide-ranging sense? Where should we locate its first beginnings and its source of inspiration? Within the standard or classic formula, 'Lord Jesus Christ, Son of God, have mercy on me', it is helpful to distinguish four constituent elements, four intertwined threads:

1 Devotion to the Holy Name 'Jesus', which is felt to act in a semi-sacramental way as a source of power and grace: in the words of *The Shepherd* of Hermas (second century), 'The Name of the Son of God is great and boundless, and it upholds the whole world'.[8] This is the basic and primary element in the Jesus Prayer.

2 The appeal for divine mercy (*eleos*), accompanied by a mingled sense of grief (*penthos*) over our sinfulness and of joy (*chara*) over God's forgiving love. The convergence of these two feelings, which are to be seen not as mutually exclusive but as complementary, is well summed up in the phrase used by St John Climacus (*c.* 570–*c.* 649), 'joy-creating grief', and more particularly in the single word of his own invention, 'joy-sorrow' (*charmolype*). (Greek, like German but unlike English, can form composite words without having to use a hyphen.)[9]

3 The discipline of frequent repetition, used as a way of attaining continual prayer.

4 The quest for inner silence or stillness (*hesychia*), in other words, for 'pure' prayer that is imageless and

3

non-discursive: in the words of Evagrius of Pontus (346–99), 'Prayer is a putting-away of thoughts'.[10] (Of course, Evagrius did not intend this as general description of prayer as such, for he would certainly have allowed an important place for liturgical prayer and the recitation of the Psalms, in which an abundance of symbols and images is employed. In this definition he is simply delineating a particular style of contemplative prayer.)

When did these four elements first emerge, and how did they come to be intertwined in the practice of the Jesus Prayer?

The veneration of the Name

Of the four elements, the most important is undoubtedly the first, reverence for the Name of God.[11] If in the experience of the Orthodox Church the Jesus Prayer has been found more effective than any other short invocation, this is precisely because it contains within it the word 'Jesus', the Holy Name of God incarnate; nor shall we begin to understand the significance of the Jesus Prayer for Orthodoxy unless we have some sense of the intrinsic force and value of the Divine Name. Fundamental to the entire tradition of the Jesus Prayer is the conviction that there is an integral connection between the name and the one who is named. The name acts as a revelation of the person. Name signifies presence; and so to call upon someone by name, with sincerity and deep feeling, is to render that person dynamically present with full reality and power.

This reverence for the name – for all names, but more especially for the Name of God – is deeply rooted in the worldview of Judaism, as of other ancient cultures. Adam's first act after his creation by God is to give names to the animals (Genesis 2.19–20): 'Whatever the man called every living creature, that was its name.' Naming is a primary and basic human activity. Without names we human beings cannot think; until we have found an appropriate name for something, we are unable clearly to apprehend that thing and to enter into relationship with it. Unnamed, anonymous, the things and persons around us remain fluid and amorphous. Names give precision, three-dimensional relief, sharpness of boundaries; names create interchange and communion. Again and again, progress in philosophy and theology, and even to some extent in science, comes through the discovery of the 'inevitable word' by which each thing can fittingly be named. By assigning names to things, we give creation a voice, rendering it articulate in praise of God. To name things is in this way a creative act, an expression of the divine image that is in each of us. When Adam in Paradise bestows names on the animals, he is fulfilling his distinctively human vocation to serve as steward and high priest of the creation.

The importance of the name is evident likewise on occasions when someone refuses to disclose his name, as happens in the case of the mysterious visitor who wrestles with Jacob (Genesis 32.29), or of the angel who tells Manoah and his wife about the imminent birth of their child Samson (Judges 13.6, 17–18). Because knowledge of the name implies relationship, to reveal one's name to another is to enter into contact with that person, and in some measure to give him or her power over oneself; hence the need at times to keep one's name secret. Since the name expresses the distinctive mystery of each person, a change of name signifies a decisive transition in our life, an entry into a radically new situation, as when Abram becomes Abraham (Genesis 17.5), when Jacob becomes Israel (Genesis 32.38), when Saul becomes Paul (Acts 13.9), and when we receive a new name in the age to come (Revelation 2.17). That is why a monk or nun is given at monastic profession a different name, usually not of their own choosing.

If all this is true in the case of ordinary human names, then it is also true – in a far more potent way – in the case of the Name of God. The revelation of the Divine Name to Moses at the burning bush marks a crucial stage in the history of salvation (Exodus 3.13–15). In the Ten Commandments and throughout the Jewish Law the profanation of God's Name is severely condemned (Exodus 20.7; Leviticus 18.21; 19.12; 21.6; 22.2, 32; Deuteronomy 5.11). The Name of the Lord is 'from everlasting' (Isaiah 63.16), 'a strong tower' (Proverbs 18.10), 'great in might' (Jeremiah 10.6). Moreover, the Name is a source not only of strength but equally of joy and healing: it is 'perfume' or 'oil of myrrh' poured out (Song of Songs 1.3). Summing up the Jewish devotion to the Holy Name, the last book in the Old Testament, Malachi, affirms: 'From the rising of the sun to its setting my name is great among the nations' (Malachi 1.11).

This Hebraic understanding of the Name passes with undiminished force from the Old Testament to the New. Evil spirits are cast out through the Name of Jesus (Matthew 7.22; Mark 9.38; 16.17), and miracles of healing are performed in his Name (Acts 3.6; 4.10, etc.); for the Name is power. Equally, it is through the Name of Jesus that our sins are forgiven (Luke 24.47), and it is into his Name (Acts 19.5) or into the Name of all three persons of the Holy Trinity (Matthew 28.19) that the Christian is baptized. In the Lord's Prayer, brief though it is, a special clause is devoted to the holiness of the Divine Name (Matthew 6.9).

While the power of the Name is a *leitmotif* throughout the entire New Testament, there are three passages in particular where it is especially emphasized. The first is at the Lord's Supper, when Christ instructs the disciples to pray 'in my Name'; evidently this is something that they have not done hitherto, and it marks a fresh and momentous advance in their relationship with him (John 16.23–24). The second is when, in the Spirit-filled weeks immediately after Pentecost, St Peter proclaims to the Jewish authorities that there is salvation only in 'the Name of Jesus Christ of Nazareth' (Acts 4.10–12). The third is when St Paul instructs the Philippians, 'At the Name of Jesus every knee should bend' (Philemon 2:10).

The Jesus Prayer, then, as a prayer invoking God by his Holy Name, is heir to a rich and ancient tradition extending throughout the Old and New Testaments. At the same time the Jesus Prayer invokes, not merely the Name of God in general, but specifically the name of God incarnate, the name that was given to the second person of the Trinity by his foster-father St Joseph after his human birth in Bethlehem. And this name 'Jesus' has a clear and precise meaning: it signifies 'salvation of Yahveh' or 'Yahveh is salvation'. As the angel says to Joseph before the birth of Christ: 'You are to name him Jesus, for he will save his people from their sins' (Matthew 1.21).

Those who employ the Jesus Prayer, then, are conscious that they are speaking in personal terms to him who is their personal Saviour. The Jesus Prayer is not merely a rhythmic mantra, designed to produce concentration or relaxation, but in a direct and explicit way it is a confession of faith in Jesus Christ as Son of God and Saviour. Without such faith, there can be no true offering of the Jesus Prayer, and it becomes no more than a 'vain repetition' (Matthew 6.7). The Name is power, but a purely mechanical repetition will achieve little or nothing. The Jesus Prayer is not a magic spell, but needs to be spoken with 'fear, faith and love', as a great spiritual teacher in Tsarist Russia, St Theophan the Recluse (1815–94), firmly insists:

> The Jesus Prayer is not some talisman. Its power comes from faith In the Lord, and from a deep union of the mind and the heart with him . . . A mere repetition of the words does not signify anything . . . It constitutes only the extreme outer limit of the work.
>
> The essential thing is to stand consciously in the presence of the Lord, with fear, faith and love.[12]

The Jesus Prayer, as well as drawing in this general way upon the reverence for the Divine Name to be found throughout Scripture, is based more particularly upon two prayers found in the Gospels. The first is the prayer of the blind man Bartimaeus, who cries out to Jesus as he enters Jericho: 'Jesus, Son of David, have mercy on me' (Mark 10.47; Luke 18.38; cf. Matthew 20.30). In Christian usage it is natural that we should call upon the Saviour with his full titles 'Lord' and 'Christ' as well as 'Jesus', and that we should address him not merely as 'Son of David' but as 'Son of God'. In this way the standard formula of the Jesus Prayer is a direct development from the prayer of the blind man of Jericho.

The second petition in the Gospels that recalls the Jesus Prayer is the prayer of the publican, 'God be merciful to me the sinner' (Luke 18.13). Here the parallel is less exact: the name

'Jesus' does not occur, and the verb employed is *hilastheti* ('be merciful', 'be propitious') and not *eleison* ('have mercy'). But when the Jesus Prayer is said in the expanded penitential form, 'have mercy on me the sinner', it certainly calls to mind the publican as well as Bartimaeus. Significantly, both in the prayer of the publican and in the Jesus Prayer, the Greek has 'the sinner' (*to hamartalo*), not merely 'a sinner'. In the Jesus Prayer, I speak to God as if I were the only sinner in the whole world. I speak, not about the sins of others, but solely about my own. I make no comparisons. I do not look sideways.

Such, then, is the scriptural background to the Jesus Prayer, and such the far-reaching significance of the first of our four intertwined strands, devotion to the Holy Name. Let us now focus more precisely upon our main question: how did it all start? How and when did the Jesus Prayer emerge as a distinct spiritual way in the Christian East? Let us try to begin at the beginning.

Arrow prayers in the Egyptian desert

Orthodox writers in the past have often traced the origins of the Jesus Prayer back to Christ himself. They claim that our Lord taught the Jesus Prayer to the apostles, and that it is to this Prayer that St Paul refers when he says, 'I would rather speak five words with my mind than ten thousand words in an [unknown] tongue' (1 Corinthians 14.19). According to St Paissy Velichkovsky (1722–94), the 'five words' of which St Paul is speaking are 'Lord Jesus Christ, have mercy on me' (the standard formula without the clause 'Son of God'), which amounts to exactly five words in Greek and Slavonic.[13] But, apart from this biblical reference – which is at best cryptic – in the first three centuries of the Christian era there is in fact no clear allusion to anything that may be termed the Jesus Prayer.

If we seek to identify the *milieu* in which the Jesus Prayer originated, a more promising place to look is fourth-century Egyptian monasticism, more particularly as found in the deserts of Nitria and Scetis.[14] It was here that there emerged the nucleus of what came later to be known as the *Sayings of the Desert Fathers* – the *Apophthegmata Patrum* or the *Gerontikon* – from which we shall often have occasion to quote. The monks of Nitria and Scetis followed a semi-eremitic way of life. They dwelt neither in complete seclusion, as the hermit St Antony the Great had done for much of his life, nor yet in fully organized coenobitic communities such as those established by St Pachomius. Instead, they were settled in scattered monastic cottages, usually with between two and six monks living together under the spiritual guidance of an older monk, known as the *abba* ('father') or *geron* ('elder') of the little group. Their way of life was simple. Initially they had no formal vows and no written rule; their daily liturgical office was brief and basic. They supported themselves by manual labour, usually of a plain and repetitive kind, such as basket-making or the plaiting of rush mats.

How, then, was the monk to occupy his mind, as he performed this uniform and monotonous work? Now the Fathers of Nitria and Scetis were deeply concerned that the monk's mind should indeed be occupied. Inspired by St Paul's ideal, 'Pray without ceasing' (1 Thessalonians 5.17), they longed to maintain continual prayer in as literal a manner as possible. As the *Sayings of the Desert Fathers* declare: 'A monk who prays only when he stands up for prayer is not really praying at all.'[15] But how could unceasing prayer of this kind be achieved in practice?

One possible solution, which was widely adopted by the Fathers of Nitria and Scetis, was to recite during their times of work passages from Scripture, and especially from the Psalms, which they knew by heart. A refinement of this was to repeat, not extended sections of the Bible, but a single verse or phrase, which was said over and over again, and which in this way imprinted itself ever more deeply upon the monk's consciousness. This practice has come to be known as 'monologic prayer' or *monologia*, that is to say, prayer of a single *logos*, of a single word or phrase.[16] In this way the monk combined work and prayer: in the words of St Theophan the Recluse, 'The hands at work, the mind and heart with God'.[17] More exactly, work and prayer were not simply combined but identified: the work itself was turned into prayer.

In the fourth-century Egyptian desert, a variety of these brief 'monologic' prayers is to be found. No single formula enjoys marked predominance, nor is any special emphasis given to the Name of Jesus, although it occurs in a few of the formulas. Often the phrases that are employed are strongly penitential. Abba Lucius, for example, used the opening verse of Psalm 50 [51]: 'Have mercy upon me, O God, according to your great mercy, and according to the multitude of your compassions blot out my offence.'[18] Abba Apollo, guilty in his youth of an exceptionally horrifying sin, repeated the words: 'As man, I have sinned; as God, forgive.'[19] But not all the formulas express contrition. Sometimes the prayer is simply a cry for help, as in the examples given by Macarius of Egypt:

> Some people asked Abba Macarius, 'How should we pray?' 'There is no need to use a lot of words,' he replied. 'Just stretch out your hands and say, "Lord, as you will and as you know best, have mercy on me." And if the conflict grows fiercer, say "Lord, help me". He knows what we need and he shows us his mercy.'[20]

In a famous text St John Cassian (*c.* 360–*c.* 430) recommended the repetition of the opening verse of Psalm 69 [70]; again, the words are not specifically penitential:

> To preserve the continual mindfulness of God, keep these holy words always before you: *O God, come to my aid; O Lord, make haste to help me* . . . I am attacked by the passion of gluttony . . . I must say at once, *O God, come to my aid; O Lord, make haste to help me* . . . I try to read but am overcome by a headache . . . I must call out, *O God, come to my aid; O Lord, make haste to help me.* I am afflicted by insomnia . . . as I sigh and groan, I must pray, *O God, come to my aid; O Lord, make haste to help me* . . . This verse should be our constant prayer: in adversity, that we may be delivered; in prosperity, that we

may be kept safe and may not fall victim to pride. Let this verse be the unremitting occupation of your heart. At work, in every task, on a journey, do not cease to repeat it . . . Meditate on these words as you drop off into slumber; through incessant use, grow accustomed to repeat them even when asleep; let them be your first thought as you awake . . . let them accompany you all the day long.[21]

In *The Sayings of the Desert Fathers* it is in fact surprisingly difficult to find forms of monologic prayer that include the name of Jesus, although there are occasional instances: Abba Sisoes, for example, said, 'Lord Jesus, protect me from my tongue',[22] while Abba Elias used the prayer, 'Jesus, help me'.[23] But, generally speaking, in the fourth-century Egyptian desert there is as yet no specifically 'Jesus-centred' spirituality.

Here, then, there is abundant evidence for the third of our four constituent elements, the discipline of repetition. The early Desert Fathers made widespread use of what may be termed 'arrow prayers': short sentences of praise, penitence or petition, shot up to heaven like arrows. As St Augustine (354–420) puts it, 'The brethren in Egypt are said to offer frequent prayers, that are very brief and suddenly shot forth' (*brevissimas et raptim quodammodo jaculatas*).[24] Somewhat anticipating our later discussion, then, we may say that the Jesus Prayer emerges initially as one among a wide variety of such 'arrow prayers'. Only gradually does the Holy Name of Jesus gain marked pre-eminence, and this does not happen as soon as the fourth century. So far as the early Desert Fathers and Mothers are concerned, there is diversity and freedom. Each was at liberty to choose the brief formula or formulas that he or she found most helpful for frequent repetition; and, more often than not, the formula actually selected did not include the word 'Jesus'.

The second of our four constituent elements, the cry for mercy and the sense of grief (*penthos*), is also prominent in the spiritual life of the fourth-century Egyptian desert. In two of the short prayers already quoted, those of Lucius and Apollo, there is a severely penitential note: 'Have mercy upon me,

O God . . . As man, I have sinned . . . '. The same note of penitence recurs throughout *The Sayings of the Desert Fathers.* 'This is our chief work,' said St Antony, 'always to blame ourselves for our sins in God's sight.'[25] When asked what he is doing in his cell, the desert-dweller can succinctly reply, 'I am weeping over my sins',[26] for 'the monk should always have *penthos* within himself'.[27] As Abba Sisoes lay dying, the one thing that occupied his attention was the need to repent: 'I do not know whether I have even begun to repent,' he said.[28] 'The nearer someone draws to God,' stated Abba Matoes, 'the more he sees himself as a sinner. It was when Isaiah the prophet saw God, that he declared himself to be wretched and impure.'[29] Not without reason, in the Syriac tradition the monk is called a 'mourner' (*abila*).

The prominent place occupied by penitence in early monastic spirituality leads Fr Irénée Hausherr to conclude: 'The Jesus Prayer did not begin with the Name of Jesus. It had its beginning in *penthos*, in mourning, in sorrow for sin.'[30] But, while agreeing with Hausherr, it is important to add that the Jesus Prayer, as it developed from the fifth century onwards, is by no means exclusively a gloomy prayer, guilt-ridden and dominated by a sense of sin. Indeed, in the petition 'have mercy on me' (*eleison me*), the word 'mercy' (*eleos*) underlines, not merely the fact that we are sinners, but also the much more important fact that God's love is greater than our sin. The Fathers sometimes linked the words *eleos* ('mercy') and *elaion* ('oil').[31] God's mercy is nothing other than the oil of his love, poured out to heal and to restore. 'Have mercy' is not a cry of despair but an expression of trustful hope.

So the Jesus Prayer, far from being predominantly dark and heavy, is a prayer filled with light and joy. This is strikingly apparent in, for example, a writer such as St Hesychius of Sinai (?eighth–ninth century):

The more the rain falls on the earth, the softer it makes it; similarly, the more we call upon Christ's Holy Name, the greater the rejoicing and exultation that it brings to the earth of our heart.

To invoke Jesus continually with a longing full of sweetness and joy is to fill the air of the heart with gladness and tranquillity.

Truly blessed is the one whose mind and heart cling as closely to the Jesus Prayer and to the ceaseless invocation of his Name as air to the body or flame to the candle. The sun rising over the earth creates the daylight; and the venerable and Holy Name of the Lord Jesus, shining continually in the mind, gives birth to countless thoughts radiant as the sun.[32]

'Be still, and know that I am God'

There is, then, clear evidence in the fourth-century Egyptian desert for the second and third of our four constituent elements: for the appeal for divine mercy and for the discipline of repetition. What of the fourth element, the quest for inner stillness (*hesychia*)?

This is certainly to be found in the writings of one who was indeed a fourth-century Desert Father, although not typically such: Evagrius of Pontus, admirer of Origen and disciple of the Cappadocian Fathers, who spent the last seventeen years of his life in Nitria and the nearby Cellia. Reacting sharply against the rationalism of Eunomius and the Anomoeans (the extreme Arian group prominent in the 360s and 370s), the Cappadocians had maintained that God's essence lies beyond human understanding; his innermost nature cannot be apprehended by the human mind or expressed in human language. 'It is easier to measure the whole ocean with a tiny cup', said St Basil the Great (*c.* 330–79), 'than to grasp the ineffable greatness of God with the human intellect.'[33] Following the Cappadocians, Evagrius in his turn insisted upon the divine mystery; as he put it: 'God cannot be grasped by the intellect. For if he could be so grasped, he would not be God.'[34]

Evagrius, like St Basil's younger brother St Gregory of Nyssa (*c.* 330–*c.*395), applied this apophatic understanding of God to the doctrine of prayer. Since the Deity is a mystery beyond our comprehension, at the higher levels of prayer we should strive to lay aside all images, words and intellectual concepts, and to approach God with what Evagrius termed a 'naked mind'. We are to seek a state of 'pure prayer' – prayer, that is to say, which is pure not merely from sinful images and thoughts but from all images and thoughts whatsoever. So Evagrius wrote: 'When you are praying, do not shape within yourself any image of the Deity, and do not let your intellect be stamped with the impress of any form; but in a non-material way, approach him who is non-material.'[35] He then summed up his teaching in words that we have already cited: 'Prayer is a putting-away of thoughts.'[36]

There is thus no doubt that Evagrius was deeply concerned with the quest for *hesychia*, for inner stillness or silence of the heart. He wanted his disciples to advance, when praying, from multiplicity to simplicity, from discursive argumentation to unitive awareness, from talking and thinking about God to being with him. But did he propose any practical method or technique whereby this non-iconic, apophatic prayer might be attained? It does not appear that he did. He laid no special emphasis upon the third of our four constituent elements, the discipline of repetition. It is true that in his treatise *On Prayer* he said, without developing the point, 'At the time of trials, use a brief but intense prayer';[37] and in his treatise *Antirrheticus* ('The Contradictor') he suggested short biblical texts with which we may rebut the temptations of the devil. But he failed to develop any detailed teaching about the practice of 'monologic' prayer; nor did he suggest that the repetition of 'arrow prayers' might be used as a way of entry into prayer that is non-iconic and free from discursive thinking.

In summary, then, we may conclude that in the desert spirituality of the fourth century three out of our four constituent elements are clearly in evidence: the appeal for mercy and a strong sense of mourning (*penthos*), the second strand; the discipline of frequent repetition, the third strand; and the quest for *hesychia* or stillness, the fourth strand. But the first strand, devotion to the Holy Name of Jesus, is largely or entirely absent; it would be premature to speak at this stage of the Jesus Prayer. Moreover, Evagrius, when insisting upon the 'putting-away of thoughts', did not attempt to establish any connection between the third strand and the fourth.

What the Desert Fathers and Evagrius omitted to do was effected half a century later by a little-known yet profoundly significant writer, St Diadochus of Photice. Diadochus placed the Holy Name of Jesus at the centre of his teaching upon prayer; and at the same time he regarded the constant repetition of the Name as the best means of attaining inner stillness. He is the vital and decisive catalyst in the spirituality of the Name. It is with him that the history of the Jesus Prayer really commences.[38]

'Give it nothing but the prayer "Lord Jesus . . . "'

Little is known about the life and personality of St Diadochus. Born around 400, dead before 486, he is the author of a 'century', a series of a hundred chapters, entitled *On Knowledge and Discernment* (the title varies in the manuscripts).[39] This work seems to be intended for monks, and so it is possible that at one stage Diadochus was superior in a monastic community. In later life he became bishop of Photice in Epirus (North Greece). In his teaching he was directly influenced by Evagrius, but he combined the systematic Evagrian approach with the warmer, more experiential and more 'affective' spirit to be found in the Macarian *Homilies* (late fourth century).[40]

In at least eight out of his hundred chapters, Diadochus speaks specifically about the 'remembrance' or 'invocation' of the Name of Jesus. The invocation of the Name is not something peripheral that he merely mentions in passing, but is one of the main themes of his treatise. It is true that he discusses many other topics as well, for he nowhere isolates the Jesus Prayer or treats it simply as a 'technique', but always sets it in the context of the total practice of the Christian life. Yet we are fully justified in saying of Diadochus that, for the first time in the history of Greek patristic theology, we have before us a 'Jesus-centred' way of prayer.

Diadochus provides a particular formula for the invocation of the Name: 'Lord Jesus' (*Kyrie Iesou*). It is unclear whether he intended a further phrase to follow these two initial words, as is the case with the formula used by Abba Philemon. There is, however, nothing in Diadochus to suggest that he had in view the use of the Name 'Jesus' entirely on its own. It is certainly to be accompanied by the title 'Lord', and perhaps by other words as well.[41]

Without any doubt, then, we find in Diadochus the first of our four constituent elements, devotion to the Holy Name Jesus. The second element, however, the cry for mercy and the sense of grief and mourning (*penthos*), is less clearly evident in his hundred chapters *On Knowledge and Discernment*. Admittedly, he does not fail to stress the need for 'godly sorrow' (see 2 Corinthians 7.10) and 'active tears',[42] and he speaks at some length about the experience of feeling abandoned by God, which the aspirant advancing on the spiritual way cannot expect to avoid.[43] But on the whole he sees the Jesus Prayer as a source of joy, light and love. So, referring to the invocation of the Name, he writes characteristically: 'This is the pearl of great price which someone can acquire by selling all that he has, and so experience the inexpressible joy of making it his own';[44] 'We have need of the Spirit's aid so that all our thoughts may be concentrated and gladdened by his inexpressible sweetness;'[45] and 'Grace illumines our whole being with a deeper awareness, warming us with great love of God.'[46] Diadochus is never sentimental, but he is not dour.

While the second element, *penthos*, is not strongly in evidence, the third element, the discipline of repetition, is very heavily emphasized by Diadochus. He is acutely aware of the commandment 'Pray without ceasing' (1 Thessalonians 5.17). We are to 'call ceaselessly upon the Lord Jesus',[47] and to 'meditate unceasingly upon this glorious and Holy Name' in the depths of our heart.[48] The remembrance of the Lord Jesus is to be 'our only study and our ceaseless task':

> If we wish to cleanse our heart, we should keep it continually aflame through practising the remembrance of the Lord, making this our only study and our ceaseless task. If we desire to free ourselves from our corruption, we ought to pray not merely from time to time but at all times; we should give ourselves always to prayer, keeping watch over our intellect even when outside places of prayer. When someone

is trying to purify gold, and allows the fire of the furnace to die down even for a moment, the material which he is purifying will harden again. So, too, someone who merely practises the remembrance of God from time to time loses through lack of continuity what he hopes to gain through his prayer. It is the mark of one who truly loves holiness that he continually burns up what is worldly in his heart through practising the remembrance of God.[49]

The effect of this faithful and uninterrupted repetition will be that the Jesus Prayer grows ever more habitual and spontaneous, rising to our lips without any conscious effort on our part, present in our mind before we have become aware that it is there. In this connection Diadochus uses the image of a little child calling instinctively on its father:

A mother teaches her child to repeat with her the word 'father', instead of prattling in his usual way, until she has formed in him the habit of calling for his father even in his sleep. In the same way grace helps the soul, sharing in its meditation and crying out with it the prayer 'Lord Jesus'.[50]

The Jesus Prayer, in other words, is to become through frequent repetition not just something that we do but something that we are – as much an instinctive part of ourselves as the drawing in of our breath and the beating of our heart. To use the terminology of St Theophan the Recluse, it is to become 'self-acting'. The nineteenth-century Russian work *The Way of a Pilgrim* provides a striking illustration of this. After the anonymous Pilgrim had been reciting the Jesus Prayer for some time, he found that, as he regained consciousness in the morning, the Prayer was already 'saying itself' within him, before he had become fully awake. As he puts it, 'Early one morning the Prayer woke me up'.[51]

Diadochus also speaks of the Jesus Prayer spreading in this way from the conscious to the unconscious level. He points out that, as we are dropping off to sleep, we are particularly vulnerable to demonic attacks. At this moment, while we are in 'a light kind of sleep', we can find protection in the Jesus Prayer:

> When our intellect begins to perceive the grace of the Holy Spirit, then Satan, too, importunes the soul with a sense of deceptive sweetness in the quiet times of the night, when we fall into a light kind of sleep. If the intellect at that time cleaves fervently to the remembrance of the glorious and Holy Name of the Lord Jesus and uses it as a weapon against Satan's deception, he gives up this trick.[52]

In this way, with God's help, we can continue the invocation of the Name even while asleep: 'I sleep, but my heart keeps vigil' (Song of Songs 5.2).

Along with the first and the third of our four constituent elements, Diadochus attaches central significance also to the fourth element, the quest for *hesychia*, for inner stillness and non-iconic prayer. Following Evagrius, he insists that when praying we should strive to lay aside all images, thoughts and concepts. But how is this to be done? In the words of one who was probably a contemporary of Diadochus, St Mark the Monk (*alias* Mark the Hermit or the Ascetic): 'The rational intellect cannot rest idle.'[53] Diadochus agrees: our human mind has, as he puts it, an innate 'need for activity' (*entrecheia*). It is useless to say to ourselves, 'Stop thinking'; we might as well say 'Stop breathing'. It does not lie in our power to halt the flow of our thoughts by a simple act of will. We cannot just reach out an invisible hand and switch off the inner television set.

What, then, is the solution? Diadochus answers that, although we cannot by a mere exertion of will-power force ourselves to stop thinking, what we can do is to assign to our ever-active minds a specific task that is at the same time straightforward and uncomplicated: the constant reiteration of the Holy Name. The invocation 'Lord Jesus', repeated over and over again, will help to dissociate us from our wandering thoughts. The extreme simplicity of the Prayer, combined with the discipline of repetition, will enable us gradually to overcome our inner fragmentation. It will unify us, focussing us upon a single centre, the Lord Jesus. Our mind will continue to wander astray; but, whenever it does so, we can bring it back gently yet firmly to the centre – to the Lord Jesus Christ himself. Let our spiritual strategy be positive, not negative. Let us not waste our energy in fighting the distractions, but let us concentrate all our attention and our love upon the person of Jesus.

Thus the Jesus Prayer is an oral prayer, a prayer in words (although the words need not be spoken aloud, but may merely be articulated in an inward way). Yet, because the words are few and simple, and because they are constantly repeated, the Prayer leads us beyond words into silence; or rather, it enables us to find the silence that is hidden in the words.

As Diadochus states in a key passage:

> The intellect requires of us imperatively some task, which will satisfy its need for activity. For the complete fulfilment of its purpose we should give it nothing but the prayer 'Lord Jesus'. 'No one', it is written, 'can say "Lord Jesus" except in the Holy Spirit' (1 Cor. 12.3). Let the intellect continually concentrate on these words within its inner shrine with such intensity that it is not turned aside to any mental images.
>
> Those who meditate unceasingly upon this glorious and Holy Name in the depths of their heart can sometimes see the light of their own intellect . . . Then the Lord awakens in the soul a great love for His glory; for when the intellect with fervour of heart maintains persistently its remembrance of that precious Name, then that Name implants in us a constant love for its goodness, since there is nothing now that stands in the way.[54]

'We should give it nothing but the prayer "Lord Jesus",' states Diadochus. Here we note a movement from diversity to uniformity. Whereas in the fourth-century Egyptian desert there was a variety of 'arrow prayers', and each person was left free to choose the formula that she or he found most helpful, Diadochus is now proposing a single and unvarying invocation.

Indeed, it is precisely this unchanging character of the invocation that leads the spiritual aspirant to non-iconic prayer. By repeating one and the same phrase over and over again, we prevent our intellect from being 'turned aside to any mental images' and bring it to a state of single-pointed concentration. *Monologia* leads to *hesychia*.

In the passage just quoted, Diadochus makes it clear that the Jesus Prayer is to be recited with or by the intellect (*nous*), and also that the meditation on the Holy Name takes place in the depths of the heart (*kardia*). Here Diadochus is drawing upon both Evagrius and the Macarian *Homilies*. In emphasizing the intellect, he is following Evagrius, who defines prayer as 'communion of the intellect with God'.[55] But, when speaking of the depths of the heart, he is influenced by the *Homilies*, in which the heart is understood as the centre of the human person, the meeting-place of the human person with God.[56] Summarizing Diadochus, then, it may be said that the Jesus Prayer is offered by the intellect in the heart.

The Jesus Prayer, Diadochus states in this same passage, leads by God's grace to a vision of light: 'Those who meditate unceasingly upon this glorious and Holy Name in the depths of their heart can sometimes see the light of their own intellect.' Evagrius also speaks about a vision of light of the intellect.[57] Evidently both Evagrius and Diadochus have in view the vision of a light that is natural and created, although non-physical; through prayer we become aware of our own inherent luminosity. But, in addition to this, both Evagrius and Diadochus allude to another and higher vision, the vision of a light that is supranatural, uncreated and divine. Thus Diadochus states at one point, 'We devote ourselves unerringly to the contemplation of the divine, beholding the world of light in an air filled with light';[58] and he speaks of being 'strongly energized by the divine light'.[59] These statements are not very explicit, and there is no doubt that Diadochus is being deliberately reticent. In general he is suspicious of visionary experiences.[60]

Levels of personhood

'By the intellect in the heart': what exactly does this mean? On what level of personhood does the Jesus Prayer function?

To understand Diadochus aright, it is necessary to keep carefully in view the distinctive meaning of the two words 'heart' (*kardia*) and 'intellect' (*nous*) in the tradition of the Christian East.[61] 'Heart' means, not just the emotions and affections, but the moral and spiritual centre of the entire human person. The heart is the seat of wisdom, memory and deep reflection, the dwelling-place of the Holy Spirit. 'Intellect', by contrast, signifies not only and not primarily the reasoning brain, but more profoundly the power of inner vision and of intuitive understanding whereby we apprehend truth not just through discursive thinking but with a sudden flash of direct insight. When, therefore, Diadochus says that meditation upon the Name takes place in the depths of the heart, he means within the innermost centre of the total Self, within the hidden *temenos* where our created personhood comes face to face with the uncreated Trinity and is enfolded by it. And when he says that the Jesus Prayer is recited by the intellect, he means at a level transcending images, words and rational concepts, in a non-discursive manner, through a direct and unmediated experience of the divine presence – not by thinking about God, but simply by being with him.

This makes clear what the Jesus Prayer is not. First, the Jesus Prayer does not work primarily on the level of the imagination (in Greek, *phantasia*). It is not a form of discursive or imaginative meditation, similar to the Ignatian or Salesian methods in the Counter-Reformation West. In reciting the Jesus Prayer, we are not to think deliberately about particular incidents in Christ's life, or about particular statements or teachings of his; for this would defeat our purpose, which is the 'putting-away of thoughts'. We are simply to have a sense of the *total presence* of Christ.

Second, the Jesus Prayer does not appeal to the will; it is not a method of wrestling with our problems and working out a solution to them. In an indirect manner, it is true, we may find that after saying the Jesus Prayer the burden of our anxieties has somehow grown lighter, and that we have begun to see a way forward through our difficulties. But, if that happens, it is precisely because during the time of prayer we were not thinking consciously about our problems, but had turned the whole of our attention to the Lord Jesus.

Third, the Jesus Prayer does not involve a deliberate use of our reasoning brain (in Greek, *dianoia*). While saying the Prayer, we do not seek to develop inner arguments about obscure points of theology. The purpose of the Jesus Prayer is not logical analysis but invocation, not abstract hypotheses but personal encounter. Having recited the Jesus Prayer for thirty minutes or an hour, we shall not find that we know a whole series of new facts *about* Jesus. But we may find that we *know Jesus* better.

Fourth, the Jesus Prayer makes use of the emotions, but it is not fundamentally a prayer of the feelings, an 'affective' prayer in the Western sense. The Jesus Prayer is indeed to be said with a vivid awareness of the Saviour's immediate presence, and with an *élan* of warm and tender love towards him. It may also be accompanied by tears; but, if it is, we need to exercise keen discernment so as to ensure that the tears are genuinely spiritual and grace-given, and not the result of our own sentimentality and over-excitement. The Prayer is to be said with sobriety and peacefulness, not with a strained and anxious vehemence. We are not to shout inwardly as we articulate the words, but the Prayer is to be like a gently running stream: in the words of St Paissy Velichkovsky, it should flow 'as water flows from a spring'.[62]

If not primarily with the imagination, the will, the reasoning brain, or the emotions, then with what faculty or level of our personhood do we recite the Jesus Prayer? Diadochus replies: *With the intellect*: that is, with the spirit rather than the reasoning brain; with our God-given capacity for intuitive vision; with what St Isaac the Syrian (seventh century) terms 'simple cognition'.[63] Also, *in the heart*: that is, with the totality of ourselves, spirit, soul and body, integrated in harmony; with the deep Self, with the ground of our being, where our created personhood meets Christ and the Spirit.

There remains a further point to be considered before we say farewell to Diadochus. To many of us, the affirmation that 'Prayer is the putting-away of thoughts' will appear a hard saying. When we try to lay aside all images, concepts and thoughts, do we not become frustrated and confused? 'Pure' prayer seems to lie far beyond our present capabilities. This is not a new difficulty. At the time of the Anthropomorphite Controversy in the Egyptian desert (399–400), when the more educated monks argued that it was an error to attribute human characteristics to the transcendent God, many of the simple Coptic brethren felt altogether bewildered when told that the Deity is not an old man with a long white beard up in the sky. 'Alas! Woe is me!' cried out one of them, Abba Serapion. 'They have taken my God away from me, and I have no one to hold on to, nor do I know whom to worship or to address.'[64] People today feel equally disoriented on being told that the Jesus Prayer is an apophatic, non-iconic prayer. How is it possible to avoid 'turning aside to mental images'?

To such people two things may be said. First, Evagrius speaks of a 'putting-away' (*apothesis*) of thoughts: not a violent uprooting, not a savage expulsion, but a gentle shedding, a gradual yet progressive detachment. Of course, images and distracting thoughts will recur. Let us not be discouraged by this. Let us not confront these thoughts and images with angry indignation, but let us quietly let them go. Second, our approach should be not so much negative as affirmative. Let us concentrate, not on what we are to get rid of, but on what we are to acquire. Let us not say, to ourselves and to others, 'Empty yourself of all thoughts and images'. Let us rather say: 'Fill yourself with a sense of joyful wonder, with an awareness of Christ's light and love'. Do not think about the distractions; think only of the Lord Jesus. Do not ask, 'How far have I progressed in expelling all wandering thoughts?' Simply say the Name of Jesus with warm tenderness of heart. Do not think about the fact that you are praying. Think only of him.

Such then is the distinctive contribution that Diadochus makes to the evolution of the Jesus Prayer. It is basically a double contribution. First, he sets the Name of Jesus at the centre of his teaching upon prayer (strand 1). Second, he combines the desert practice of 'monologic' prayer – the repetition of a single phrase (strand 3) – with the Evagrian understanding of 'pure' prayer (strand 4). In this way he provides what Evagrius fails to supply: a practical method whereby we may attain apophatic prayer.

With the teaching of Diadochus the practice of the Jesus Prayer is fully established in all its essentials. In the later Byzantine and in the modern Greek and Russian tradition, these essentials are not fundamentally altered, but they are merely deepened and enriched. More particularly, in the Palaeologan era St Gregory Palamas (1296–1359) and his disciples linked the Jesus Prayer with the vision of the divine light that shone from Christ at his transfiguration on Mount Tabor. The recitation of the Prayer, so they believed, brings the hesychast to an experience of uncreated Taboric glory. Diadochus, however, as we have seen, refers briefly to this vision of divine light; thus the later Byzantine teaching about the Jesus Prayer and the light of the transfiguration is at least implicit in his work, although not explicitly developed.

Shortly before the time of Palamas, there was another significant development in the history of the Jesus Prayer. Byzantine writers, from the thirteenth century onwards, propose the use of a physical technique in connection with the Prayer, involving a specific posture, control of the breathing, and concentration upon different psychosomatic centres of energy, in particular the heart. There is nothing about this in Diadochus, although there are possible hints about the co-ordination of the Prayer with the rhythm of the breathing in John Climacus and Hesychius.[65] Also, during the later Byzantine or early post-Byzantine period, at a date hard to determine, it becomes customary during the reciting of the Jesus Prayer to employ a prayer-rope or rosary (Greek *komvoschoinion*, Slavonic *tchotki*). Again, Diadochus does not mention this (nor indeed do fourteenth-century writers such as Gregory of Sinai, Gregory Palamas or the Xanthopouloi).

All this, however, does not affect our point that with Diadochus the traditional teaching about the Jesus Prayer is already present in all its essentials. For the physical technique and the use of a prayer-rope are no more than useful accessories; they are not essential parts of the Jesus Prayer. The essence of the Jesus Prayer consists in the repeated invocation of the Holy Name of Jesus, and this can be practised in its fullness without the use of any outward technique whatsoever.

Let us conclude with a final word from the Bishop of Photice. 'Nothing', says St Diadochus, 'is more poor and mean than a mind which philosophizes about God when it is in fact outside him.'[66] Surely this is a warning to be noted by all who write books concerning spirituality, and by all who read such books. Theory is valueless without practice. Prayer is a matter of lived experience.

Notes

1 'A Discourse on Abba Philemon': Greek text in *Philokalia ton Ieron Neptikon*, vol. 2 (Athens, Astir, 1958), p. 244, lines 36–39; tr. G. E. H. Palmer, Philip Sherrard and Kallistos Ware, *The Philokalia: The Complete Text 2* (London and Boston, Faber & Faber, 1981), p. 348. On the uncertain date of this work, see Basile Krivochéine, 'Date du texte traditionnel de la "Prière de Jésus"', *Messager de l'Exarchat du Patriarche Russe en Europe Occidentale* 7–8 (1951), pp. 55–59.

2 On the evolution of the Jesus Prayer, consult Irénée Hausherr, *Noms du Christ et Voies d'Oraison* (Orientalia Christiana Analecta 157; Rome, Pontificium Institutum Orientalium Studiorum, 1960); tr. Charles Cummings, *The Name of Jesus* (Cistercian Studies Series 44; Kalamazoo, MI, Cistercian Publications, 1978). See also 'Un Moine de l'Eglise d'Orient' ('A Monk of the Eastern Church', Archimandrite Lev Gillet), *La Prière de Jésus*, 4th edn (Paris, Editions de Chevetogne/Livre de Vie, 1963); revised English translation, *The Jesus Prayer*, ed. Kallistos Ware (Crestwood, NY, St Vladimir's Seminary Press, 1987). Both these works are now out of date. For a brief treatment, see Kallistos Ware, *The Power of the Name: The Jesus Prayer in Orthodox Spirituality* (Fairacres Publication 43, rev. edn; Oxford, SLG Press, 1986); and, by the same author, 'The Origins of the Jesus Prayer: Diadochus, Gaza, Sinai', in Cheslyn Jones, Geoffrey Wainwright and Edward Yarnold (eds), *The Study of Spirituality* (London, SPCK, 1986), pp. 175–84.

3 This is the form most frequently used among the Russians in the last two centuries. It first occurs, to the best of my knowledge, in the fourteenth-century *Life of St Gregory of Sinai* by Patriarch

Kallistos of Constantinople: see Kallistos Ware, 'The Jesus Prayer in St Gregory of Sinai', *Eastern Churches Review* 4.1 (1972), p. 18.

4 For the use of the form 'My Jesus' by the two Xanthopouloi in the late fourteenth century, see David Balfour, *Saint Gregory the Sinaïte: Discourse on the Transfiguration* (offprint from the journal *Theologia*; Athens, 1983), pp. 147–8; Kallistos Ware, *A Fourteenth-Century Manual of Hesychast Prayer: The Century of St Kallistos and St Ignatios Xanthopoulos* (Toronto, Canadian Institute of Balkan Studies, 1995), pp. 17–19.

5 On the Jesus Prayer in the West, consult Rama Coomaraswamy, *The Invocation of the Name Jesus as Practiced in the Western Church* (Louisville, KY, Fons Vitae, 1999).

6 See Kallistos Ware, 'The Jesus Prayer and the Mother of God', *Eastern Churches Review* 4.2 (1972), pp. 149–50.

7 A possible exception to this might be found in the writings of St Gregory of Sinai (d. 1346). Discussing various ways in which the standard formula may be abbreviated, he mentions as one possibility the phrase 'Son of God, have mercy on me'. But this last, since it does not include the actual name 'Jesus', is strictly speaking no longer a form of the Jesus Prayer. See Ware, 'The Jesus Prayer in St Gregory of Sinai', p. 12.

8 *Similitudes* 9.14.5, ed. Robert Joly (Sources Chrétiennes 53; Paris, Cerf, 1958), p. 324.

9 *The Ladder of Divine Ascent* 7 (*PG* 88:801C, 804B); tr. Colm Luibheid and Norman Russell (The Classics of Western Spirituality; New York, Ramsey, Toronto, Paulist Press, 1982), p. 137.

10 *On Prayer* 70 (71) (*PG* 79:1181C); tr. Palmer, Sherrard and Ware, *The Philokalia: The Complete Text* 1 (London and Boston, Faber & Faber, 1979), p. 64. (The translators here render, 'Prayer means the shedding of thoughts'.)

11 The fundamental Orthodox work on the theology of the Holy Name is by Archpriest Sergei Bulgakov (1871–1944), *Filosofia Imeni*, ed. Léon Zander (Paris, YMCA Press, 1953); tr. Constantin Andronnikov, *Philosophie du verbe et du nom* (Collection Sophia; Lausanne, L'Age d'Homme, 1991).

12 Quoted in Igumen Chariton of Valamo, *The Art of Prayer: An Orthodox Anthology*, tr. E. Kadloubovsky and E. M. Palmer (London, Faber & Faber, 1966), pp. 99–100.

13 See *The Art of Prayer*, p. 91.

14 For the classic description of life in Nitria, see Palladius, *The Lausiac History*, 7. For the Greek text of the main collection of the *Apophthegmata Patrum*, see *PG* 65:76–440; *The Sayings of the Desert Fathers: The Alphabetical Collection*, tr. Sister Benedicta Ward, rev. edn (London and Oxford, Mowbray, 1981). Compare Derwas J. Chitty, *The Desert a City: An Introduction to the Study of Egyptian and*

Palestinian Monasticism under the Christian Empire (Oxford, Blackwell, 1966), pp. 11–13, 29–36, 46–61, 66–74.

15 *Apophthegmata Patrum*, anonymous collection, 104, ed. F. Nau, *Revue de l'Orient Chrétien* 12 (1907), p. 402. Compare Kallistos Ware, 'Pray Without Ceasing: The Ideal of Continual Prayer in Eastern Monasticism', in *The Inner Kingdom* (Crestwood, NY, St Vladimir's Seminary Press, 2000), pp. 75–87.

16 See Lucien Regnault, 'La Prière Continuelle "Monologistos" dans les Apophtegmes des Pères', *Irénikon* 48 (1974), pp. 467–93; reprinted in Regnault, *Les Pères du Désert à travers leurs Apophtegmes* (Solesmes, Sablé-sur-Sarthe, 1987), pp. 113–39.

17 See Chariton of Valamo, *The Art of Prayer*, p. 92.

18 *Apophthegmata Patrum*, alphabetical collection, Lucius, 1; Ward (tr.), *Sayings*, p. 121. Here, as elsewhere, I have sometimes made my own translation from the original.

19 Apollo, 2; tr. Ward, *Sayings*, p. 36.

20 Macarius the Great, 19; Ward (tr.), *Sayings*, p. 131. Macarius does not in fact specify that these short prayers are to be frequently repeated, but they easily could be.

21 *Conference* 10.10; tr. Boniface Ramsey (Ancient Christian Writers 57; New York and Mahwah, Paulist Press, 1997), pp. 379–83.

22 Alphabetical collection, Sisoes the Great, 5; Ward (tr.), *Sayings*, p. 213.

23 Elias, 7; Ward (tr.), *Sayings*, p. 71. Nothing is said here about repetition.

24 *To Proba, Letter* 130.20 (*PL* 33:501).

25 Alphabetical collection, Antony, 4; Ward (tr.), p. 2.

26 Dioscorus, 2; Ward (tr.), p. 55.

27 Poemen, 26; Ward (tr.), p. 171.

28 Sisoes, 14; Ward (tr.), p. 215.

29 Matoes, 2; Ward (tr.), p. 143. Cf. Isaiah 6.5.

30 Hausherr, *Noms du Christ*, p. 118; Cummings, *The Name of Jesus*, p. 104.

31 See, for example, Clement of Alexandria, *The Pedagogue*, 2.8 (62.3); St John Chrysostom, *Homilies on Matthew*, 78.1 (*PG* 57:712). The etymology is dubious, but the theology is surely sound.

32 *On Watchfulness and Holiness*, 1.41, 89; 2.94 (in the continuous numbering, 41, 91, 196) (*PG* 93:1493C, 1508C, 1541CD); *Philokalia*, 1, pp. 169, 177–8, 197.

33 *On Psalm 115*, 2 (*PG* 30:105D).

34 *On the Eight Evil Thoughts* (*PG* 40:1275C) (Latin only: Evagrian authorship perhaps doubtful).

35 *On Prayer* 66 (67) (*PG* 79:1181A); *Philokalia*, 1, p. 63.

36 *On Prayer* 70 (71) (*PG* 79:1181A); *Philokalia*, 1, p. 64.

37 *On Prayer* 97 (98) (*PG* 79:1189A); *Philokalia*, 1, p. 66.

38 An older contemporary of Diadochus, St Nilus of Ancyra (active
   c. 430), in the course of his wide-ranging correspondence recommended on four occasions the 'invocation' or 'remembrance' of
   the Name of Jesus (*Letters* 2.140, 214; 3.273, 278: *PG* 79:260A,
   313D, 520B, 521BC). But these are no more than allusions made
   in passing; they do not form part of any developed teaching about
   the invocation of the Name. Diadochus has a much better claim
   than Nilus to be considered the true originator of the Jesus
   Prayer.

39 Greek text edited by Édouard des Places, *Diadoque de Photicé:
   Oeuvres Spirituelles* (Sources Chrétiennes 5 ter; Paris, Cerf, 1966),
   pp. 84–163; *Philokalia*, 1, pp. 252–96. See also Kallistos Ware, 'The
   Jesus Prayer in St Diadochus of Photice', in George Dion. Dragas,
   *Aksum – Thyateira: A Festschrift for Archbishop Methodios of Thyateira
   and Great Britain* (London, Thyateira House, 1985), pp. 557–68.

40 For a comparison between Evagrius and the Macarian *Homilies*,
   see Kallistos Ware, 'Prayer in Evagrius of Pontus and the Macarian
   Homilies', in Ralph Waller and Benedicta Ward (eds), *An Introduction to Christian Spirituality* (London, SPCK, 1999), pp. 14–30.

41 Of the two main authors who have written about the Jesus Prayer,
   'A Monk of the Eastern Church' (Lev Gillet) and Irénée Hausherr
   (see note 2), the first considers that the Jesus Prayer began with
   the use of the name 'Jesus' recited on its own; at a later date the
   invocation was gradually expanded through the addition of other
   words, and in this way what we have termed the standard formula
   eventually emerged (*La Prière de Jésus*, pp. 51–52, 72; *The Jesus
   Prayer*, pp. 71, 93). Hausherr disagrees: he argues – in my opinion,
   correctly – that, in all the early texts where a specific formula of
   invocation is to be found, the name 'Jesus' is accompanied by
   other words (Hausherr, *Noms du Christ*, p. 118; Cummings, *The
   Name of Jesus*, p. 104). Occasionally, it is true, the use of the name
   'Jesus' on its own is indeed recommended by Eastern Christian
   authors; one example is St Amvrosy of Optino (1812–91). But
   such instances are rare and late.

42 *On Knowledge and Discernment*, 60.

43 *On Knowledge and Discernment*, 86–87.

44 *On Knowledge and Discernment*, 59. Cf. Matthew 13.46.

45 *On Knowledge and Discernment*, 61.

46 *On Knowledge and Discernment*, 85.

47 *On Knowledge and Discernment*, 85.

48 *On Knowledge and Discernment*, 59.

49 *On Knowledge and Discernment*, 97.

50 *On Knowledge and Discernment*, 61.

51 *The Way of a Pilgrim*, tr. R. M. French, new edn (London, SPCK,
   1954), p. 14. Cf. the more recent translation by T. Allan Smith,

The Pilgrim's Tale, ed. Aleksei Pentkovsky (The Classics of Western Spirituality; New York and Mahwah, Paulist Press, 1999), p. 64.

52 *On Knowledge and Discernment*, 31.

53 *On Repentance*, 11; ed. Georges-Matthieu de Durand (Sources Chrétiennes 445; Paris, Cerf, 1999), p. 250.

54 *On Knowledge and Discernment*, 59.

55 *On Prayer*, 3 (*PG* 79:1168C); *Philokalia*, p. 57.

56 See, for example, *Homilies*, Collection II, ed. Hermann Dörries, Erich Klostermann and Matthias Kroeger (Patristische Texte und Studien 4; Berlin, Gruyter, 1964), 15.20; 43.7; *Pseudo-Macarius: The Fifty Spiritual Homilies and the Great Letter*, tr. George Maloney (The Classics of Western Spirituality; New York and Mahwah, Paulist Press, 1992), pp. 116, 222.

57 See, for example, *On Thoughts*, 39, 43: ed. Paul Géhin, with Claire and Antoine Guillaumont (Sources Chrétiennes 438; Paris, Cerf, 1998), pp. 286–8, 298. On the light of the intellect, see A. Guillaumont, 'La Vision de l'Intellect par Lui-même dans la Mystique Évagrienne', in A. Guillaumont, *Études sur la Spiritualité de l'Orient Chrétien* (Spiritualité Orientale 66; Bégrolles-en-Mauge, Abbaye de Bellefontaine, 1996), pp. 143–50.

58 *On Knowledge and Discernment*, 75.

59 *On Knowledge and Discernment*, 40.

60 *On Knowledge and Discernment*, 36, 40.

61 See Ware, 'Prayer in Evagrius of Pontus', pp. 14–30, especially pp. 16–17, 20–22.

62 'Field Flowers', ch. 24, in *Little Russian Philokalia*, 4, ed. New Valaam Monastery, Alaska (Platina, CA, St Herman Press; Forestville, CA, St Paisius Abbey Press, 1994), p. 89.

63 *Mystic Treatises by Isaac of Nineveh*, Homily 22, tr. A. J. Wensinck (Amsterdam, Koninklijke Akademie van Wetenschappen, 1923), p. 114.

64 John Cassian, *Conference* 10.3, tr. Ramsey, p. 373.

65 See Kallistos Ware, 'Praying with the Body: The Hesychast Method and Non-Christian Parallels', *Sobornost incorporating Eastern Churches Review* 14.2 (1992), pp. 6–35, especially p. 9.

66 *On Knowledge and Discernment*, 8.

2

THE OUR FATHER

BENEDICTA WARD

> *Our Father, who art in heaven,*
> *hallowed be thy name.*
> *Thy kingdom come.*
> *Thy will be done on earth as it is in heaven.*
> *Give us this day our daily bread.*
> *And forgive us our trespasses,*
> *as we forgive those who trespass against us.*
> *And lead us not into temptation,*
> *but deliver us from evil.*

In the Gospels of Matthew (6.9–13) and of Luke (11.2–4) we read that the disciples said to Jesus, 'Lord, teach us to pray'. His response, 'When you pray, say, "Our Father, which art in heaven",' has created the best-known of all Christian texts, the Our Father. It has formed the structure for Christian prayer ever since and there are countless commentaries on each section of it. It has been seen as the teaching of the Lord himself about prayer and has been known by innumerable people, who have used it in just that way. Known by heart, the text has become physically part of those praying, and has then continued to act as a gateway into prayer for the whole of their lives without further analysis. That is its purpose, but there is also a place for thinking about the words and for using the intellect to explore their riches. This exploration has been done by commentators from the early Church until today, and, though there is a basic similarity between them, there is also much that expresses a difference of perception in detail. I have chosen five writers as expositors of this prayer: Origen from the third century; John Cassian from the fourth; two Englishmen, the Venerable Bede and Alcuin of York, from the eighth; and Teresa of Avila from the sixteenth. I have put together first of all the general comments of each of them about the prayer itself, and have then grouped their comments together under each clause of the Our Father.

General comments

Origen (*c.* 185–254), the earliest and greatest of the early Church Fathers, wrote his commentary on the Our Father in the form of a letter, which in length seems better described by the word 'treatise', addressed to an elderly friend, Ambrose, and his wife Tatiana.[1] Such personal spiritual instruction has often taken the form of a letter, since, although such texts were meant to be a public type of literature, the more personal use of the first person singular was found to be especially appropriate for spirituality. The whole of Christian prayer was described by Origen in terms of the clauses of the Our Father and this provided the method for later writers. His commentary was formed by the style of patristic commentary on Scripture, first presenting a literal discussion of the grammar of the text, then asking what it means to the reader, and then what it tells the reader about Christ and about heaven. The whole Bible was seen as a word of God and all parts were seen to interpret every other part. So in commenting on this key prayer Origen applied different levels of understanding to each part and also set it within the whole of Scripture. He began with the grammatical and textual aspects of the passage, noticing differences between the two versions as a basis for further discussion:

> I have said enough already about the problem of prayer in general, so I will now go on to the next task, and look at the prayer given by the Lord and the power with which it is filled. First, notice that it only seems that Matthew and Luke have written the same form of prayer according to which we should pray. The words given by Matthew are as follows: Our Father, who art in heaven, hallowed be thy name. Thy kingdom come. Thy will be done on earth as it is in heaven.

Give us this day our supersubstantial bread. And forgive us our debts, as we also forgive our debtors. And lead us not into temptation, but deliver us from evil. But Luke reads thus: Father, hallowed be thy name. Thy kingdom come. Give us each day our supersubstantial bread. And forgive us our sins, for we also forgive everyone that is indebted to us. And lead us not into temptation.[2]

After discussing each phrase of the prayer in depth, at the end Origen drew the treatise together with an outline of the shape of Christian prayer as seen in the Our Father:

I am going to bring this treatise to an end by going through the essential parts of prayer. I have found scattered in the Scriptures four important aspects that need explaining, and all should organize their prayer with these as a pattern. Here are the main parts: at the beginning, at the start of prayer, wholeheartedly glorify God through Christ, who is glorified with him, in the Holy Spirit, who is praised with him. Next, thank God for all his benefits, remembering both those things that are given in general to all and those that are special to you. This thanksgiving, I think, should be followed by a sorrowful confession of sins; ask God first for healing in order to be delivered from customs that lead to sin, and ask then for forgiveness of past sins. After confession, the fourth part of prayer is petition, by which God is asked for great and heavenly gifts, for yourself and for all, for your relatives and friends; and, finally, conclude the prayer by giving glory to God through Christ in the Holy Spirit.[3]

This pattern of prayer became standard for Christian meditation, and the monk John Cassian (c. 360–435), who knew Origen's treatise, continued to comment on the prayer in a similar way. He wrote a series of *Conferences* in the form of letters addressed to Bishop Castor, Bishop Leontius and the monk Helladius, in order to help them to understand the monks under their care. These were the new monks of Gaul, and Cassian was especially involved in training those near Marseilles who wanted to follow the example of the first Christian monks. Cassian's two books, the *Institutes* and the *Conferences*, were based on his travels in Egypt, the home of early Christian monasticism, where he had talked with many of the monks in the desert. In one of the *Conferences* in particular, the ninth, which contained the second part of the teaching of Abba Isaac on prayer, Cassian commented on the Our Father. Like Origen, he saw it as containing the whole of prayer, with four stages, similar to, though not identical with, those of Origen. For Origen, it was the basic form of prayer: 'The plan of the Lord's prayer has taught us that we must always seek the condition of sonship when it says "Our Father".'[4] But for Cassian the Our Father was not the limit of prayer but the beginning, the way into 'wordless prayer':

> This prayer, although it seems to contain the fullness of perfection because it was instituted and established by the authority of the Lord himself, none the less raises his friends to that condition which we characterized previously as more sublime: that fiery and wordless prayer which is known and experienced by very few.[5]

The Lord's Prayer was here seen as the gateway into mystical states of prayer, characterized by the images of fire and of tears, which the monastic tradition saw as the signs of the work of the Holy Spirit in the soul.

In the seventh century, another monk, Bede of Wearmouth and Jarrow (673–735), also considered the Our Father to be the primary prayer for Christians among the newly converted Anglo-Saxons in England. He did not write a treatise on the Our Father, but in his commentary on the Gospel of St Luke and in his other works on the Scriptures he referred to it constantly. Like his predecessors, Bede read more than the surface meaning of the words in every part of Scripture, and this was so in his comments on the Lord's Prayer.[6] Here is an example of his method, in which he saw all parts of the Bible as one, so that part of the Old Testament can be used to illuminate the New; a sentence from the book of Samuel is connected to the gospel:

Then thou [Saul] shalt go forward from thence and thou shalt come to the plain of Tabor and there shall meet thee three men going up to God at Bethel, one carrying three kids, another carrying three loaves of bread and another carrying a bottle of wine; and they will salute thee and give thee two loaves of bread, which thou shalt receive at their hands' (1 Samuel 10.3). The disciples received bread from the hands of the Lord when he opened their understanding that they might understand the Scriptures.[7]

Bede used the same four-fold method of understanding the Bible as his predecessors and described it under the image of cooking food in different ways:

We are being nourished on food roasted on the gridiron when we understand literally, openly and without any covering the things that have been said or done to protect the health of the soul; we feed on food cooked in a frying-pan when, by frequently turning over the superficial meaning and looking at it afresh, we comprehend what there is in it that corresponds allegorically with the mysteries of Christ, what with the condition of the catholic church, and what with setting right the ways of individuals; and afterwards we search in the oven for the bread of the Word when by exertion of mind we lay hold of those mystical things in the Scriptures, that is, upon matters hidden above, which as yet we cannot see but which we hope we shall see hereafter.[8]

Bede also followed Origen, Cassian and Augustine in presenting the Our Father as the basic structure of prayer:

It is not without meaning that it is said that the Lord himself prayed and taught his disciples to pray, both because the prayer he taught contained in itself the sacrament of life (and we cannot obtain the perfection of our lives except by prayer); and also because repeatedly Luke described the Saviour as praying, which prayer he carried out not for his own sake but for ours.[9]

Having established the importance of the way of prayer presented in the Our Father, Bede then discussed the whole structure of the prayer:

> In the Gospel according to Matthew the Lord's prayer seems to contain seven petitions, three of which ask for eternal things, the remaining four for things temporal, though the last four are necessary antecedents to the attainment of the eternal goods. For when we say 'Hallowed be thy name, thy kingdom come, thy will be done on earth as it is in heaven', which some understand not unfairly as in body as well as in spirit, we ask for things that are to be enjoyed for ever; they are indeed begun in this world and grow in us as we go forward, but we hope to possess them wholly in another life for ever. But when we say, 'Give us this day our daily bread, forgive us our debts as we forgive our debtors, lead us not into temptation but deliver us from evil', who does not see that these things belong to the needs of this present life? . . . At some services only the final part of the Lord's prayer is said aloud, and this is done so that all may reply, 'But deliver us from evil.'[10]

Bede's interest in the Lord's Prayer was not so other-worldly as that of Cassian; he allowed for an earthly meaning for the petitions, not only for the sublime heights of mysticism. He was writing for those involved in ministry to a newly converted people and, moreover, he himself was accustomed to the daily public recitation of the Lord's Prayer in Latin as part of the Office; a section in the *Rule of St Benedict* recommends its recitation, which suggests that this was common monastic practice: 'Certainly the celebration of lauds and vespers must never pass by without the superior reciting the entire Lord's Prayer.'[11]

Bede was particularly concerned that this treasury of prayed theology should be available to form the structure of prayer for the whole people of God, not just for those scholars and monks who knew Latin. He wrote about this at the end of his life in his last written work, a letter to Bishop Egbert of York, an old colleague, advising him about the life of Christians in the

diocese for which he was responsible. Bede stressed the importance of seeing that the Our Father was known by heart by all,
in English where Latin was not known:

> In preaching to the people, this message more than any
> other should be proclaimed; that the catholic faith as
> contained in the Apostles' Creed and the Lord's Prayer,
> which the reading of the gospel teaches us, should be interi-
> orly memorized by all who are under your rule. All who have
> learnt Latin by constant reading have certainly learnt these
> texts as well, but as for the unlearned, that is, those who
> know only their own tongue, let them learn the texts in their
> own language and sing them accurately. This should be done
> not only by the laity, who are still living a worldly life, but also
> by any clerks and monks who are not expert in the Latin
> language. So it will come about that the whole congregation
> of believers will learn how to be full of faith and will know
> how to protect and arm themselves against the attacks of evil
> spirits by firm belief. The result will be that the whole choir
> of those who are praying to God will understand what should
> be specially sought from the mercy of God. That is why I have
> often made translations of both the Creed and the Lord's
> Prayer into English and offered them to priests who do not
> know Latin . . . Moreover, the custom of repeated prayer and
> genuflexions has taught us to sing the Lord's Prayer more
> often.[12]

No translations of the Our Father by Bede into Anglo-Saxon
are extant, but there are later versions that must have been very
close to his work, and they show how the text could be
presented faithfully but at the same time given meaning in
phrases familiar to a new culture:

Pater noster qui es in celis
Father of mankind, I pray you for healing, holy Lord in the
heavens.

sanctificetur nomen tuum.
May this your name be hallowed now, fast fixed in our minds,
redeeming Christ, fast established in our hearts.

Adveniat regnum tuum.
May your kingdom now come to us mortals, Wielder of
mighty powers, righteous Judge, and may your glorious faith
remain in our hearts for the span of our lives.

Fiat voluntas tua sicut in celo et in terra.
And may your will be fulfilled among us in the habitation of
the kingdom of earth, as clear as it is in the glory of heaven,
made both dear and lovely for ever and to eternity.

Panem nostrum cotidianum da nobis hodie
Give us now today, Lord of men, high King of the heavens,
our bread, which you sent into the world as salvation to the
souls of mankind: that is, the pure Christ, the Lord God.

et dimitte nobis debita nostra
Forgive us, Guardian of men, our guilts and sins, and pardon
our crimes, the body's wounds, and our wicked deeds,
although we often offend against you, the almighty God, in
your mercies,

sicut et nos dimittimus debitoribus nostris.
just as we pardon on earth the crimes of those who often do
wrong against us, and do not think to accuse them of their
evil deeds, in order to have eternal life.

Et ne nos inducas in temptationem
Do not lead us to punishment, to the grief of affliction, nor
to the testing, redeeming Christ, lest we, devoid of grace,
become out of enmity estranged from all your mercies.

sed libera nos a malo.
And also free us now from the evil of every fiend; we in our
hearts shall eagerly speak of thanks and glory, Prince of the

angels, true Lord of victories, because you have mercifully set us free from the bondage of hell's torments by your mighty power.

Amen.
So let it be.[13]

It was the content and inner meaning of the prayer that was to be known, not just external words; it was therefore to be said in a familiar language and also given the extra dignity of being sung by all. This advice was echoed later when Alfred the Great began to reconstruct the English Church and nation after the incursions of the Danes, and he attributed the failure of the late Anglo-Saxon Church to its not having followed this advice of Bede about seeing that the content of the prayer was absorbed through the use of translations:

> Before everything was ransacked and burned, the churches throughout England were filled with treasures and with books. Similarly, there was a great multitude serving God. They derived very little benefit from their books because they could understand nothing of them since they were not written in their own language. Therefore we have now lost the wealth as well as the wisdom, because we did not wish to set our minds on the right way.[14]

Fifty years later this approach was paralleled by another Anglo-Saxon scholar, Alcuin of York (736–804). A devoted admirer of Bede, Alcuin was an Englishman who had been taught by Bede's pupil and colleague Egbert of York. He became Master of the Cathedral School at York and was later the central figure in the Carolingian renaissance at the court of Charlemagne. Like Bede he included in his comments on the Lord's Prayer the passage already quoted from Bede on the form of the prayer, but in his comments clause by clause he was concerned with content and meaning for the praying heart. While Bede's comments are embedded in biblical exposition and homilies, Alcuin's commentary is found in the part of his work that deals with the liturgical prayer of the Church, thus giving it a corporate setting as the central prayer for Christians when they pray together.[15] Together, Bede and Alcuin presented the interior understanding of the Lord's Prayer for the English as being essential whether prayed alone or with others.

In the sixteenth century, there was another notable exposition of the Lord's Prayer by Teresa of Avila (1515–97). The founder of the Order of Discalced Carmelites, and the first woman to be given the title Doctor of the Church, she was the contemplative writer *par excellence*. She was most concerned with the exploration of prayer as a way of life, which might or might not include mystical states of prayer, and she wrote her work on the Our Father in Spanish for her nuns while she was at her new foundation of St Joseph's. At the request of these enclosed contemplative nuns, she wrote about the way of prayer they were following, concentrating in *The Way of Perfection* on vocal prayer that was common to all, and drawing from it the highest levels of contemplation. The heart of the treatise (chs 27–42; fifteen chapters out of forty-two) analyse the Our Father; these are sometimes printed separately and called the *Paternoster Treatise*.[16] For Teresa, the specific nature of Christian prayer began with the gift of God in his Son; the beginning was not the creation but the re-creation of all. She exclaims at the wonder of this claim of sonship in the first words of the prayer, given that it is the end and aim and height of perfection. She suggests that it might seem more appropriate to start at the end, with 'Deliver us from evil', since the phrase 'Our Father' is in a sense the climax of prayer rather than the beginning.[17] She also, like Origen and Cassian, saw it as being prayed by Jesus himself, as his prayer to the Father; and she goes even further than her predecessors in explaining how the whole way of mystical union is contained within it:

The heavenly perfection of this evangelical prayer is something for which we should give great praise to the Lord. It was so well composed by the good Master, my daughters, that each of us may use it in her own way. I am astounded when I consider that in its few words are contained the whole

of contemplation and perfection, so that if we study it no
other book will be necessary. In the Paternoster the Lord has
taught us the whole method of prayer and contemplation,
from the first beginnings of mental prayer to the prayerful
states of Quiet and Union.[18]

The approach of all these writers is similar; their understanding
of the Our Father is that it is primarily the prayer of Jesus
praying to the Father and including in his words all created
beings as sons in the Son. Within this new relationship, established by redemption, the whole of prayer can be found in
these words, and the prayer itself can also be a basis for the way
of mystical and contemplative union with God. Each of these
writers makes specific comments on the separate clauses of the
Our Father, some of which I have grouped together under each
phrase, to offer a sense of the interpretation most often given
to the separate sections.

Detailed comments

Our Father

Each of the commentators begins with the statement that the
fatherhood of God is conferred not only by creation but by
the adoption of mankind in the second person of the Trinity,
the Son of God:

> When we confess with our own voice that the God and Father
> of the universe is Our Father, we are affirming that we have
> in fact been taken out of our servile condition and given
> sonship by adoption.[19]

This is presented as true whenever the prayer is said, but especially so when it is used in the context of the Eucharist:

> And here the priest joins his hands and says 'Let us pray',
> and the church prays with the priest not in voice but in heart.
> In silence the heart cries to God in the ears of God, 'Our
> Father'. The only begotten Son has made us sons of God by

the font of new birth and the spirit of adoption. So when we do what he says, 'When you pray, say, "Our Father", we are acting out of obedience, not out of boldness. The sons must imitate their good father as Isaac imitated Abraham and Jacob Isaac, as he said: "Be ye holy because I the LORD your God am holy"' (Leviticus 20.26).[20]

The idea of God as a loving and present Father, who cares intimately for his children, follows from this:

> You have a good Father given you by the good Jesus; let no other father be known or referred to here. Strive, my daughters, to be such that you deserve to find comfort in him and to throw yourselves into his arms. You know that, if you are good children, he will never send you away.[21]

Who art in heaven

The second clause of the prayer, again in the present tense, affirms that 'our Father' is eternally present beyond the confines and limitations of this earthly life, not somewhere different in space but in the 'heaven' of an eternal now; the response to this realization is therefore stated in terms of a dynamic pilgrimage to him:

> Avoid with utter horror staying in the dwelling-place of this present life; here we live on earth as on a journey and are kept at a far distance from our Father. Let us instead hasten with great desire to that region in which we say that our Father dwells.[22]

The idea of life as a pilgrimage, a journey to the place where we really belong, does not locate 'heaven' as always ahead; heaven is also within the soul of everyone created in the image and likeness of God, so that God is always within us, for intimate converse:

41

We have no need to go to heaven or to speak in a loud voice; however quietly we speak he is so near that he will hear us . . . There are those who able to shut themselves up in this way within this little heaven of the soul wherein dwells the Maker of heaven and earth; they will come without fail to drink of the water of the fountain of life.[23]

Hallowed be thy name

The prayer that the name of God may be known as holy is linked by all writers with the service of Christians, in whom Christ lives and acts:

Hallowed be thy name – this is done by self-giving service by Christ in us for the sake of all. We testify that our desire and joy is the glory of the Father, since we have become imitators of him who said: 'The one who speaks of himself seeks his own glory, but the one who seeks the glory of him who sent him is true and there is no unrighteousness in him (John 7.18).'[24]

The question of any incongruity in asking for something that already exists, since the name of God is by definition holy, is resolved by underlining the continuing hallowing of the earthly life of Christians, as they strive always to become what they already are:

The name of God is holy, so why do we say, 'Hallowed by thy name'? When we are born again by water and the Spirit at baptism, we are made holy in the name of God almighty when the priest says, 'I baptize you in the name of the Father and of the Son and of the Holy Spirit'. So we pray that the holiness that was created in us then at baptism by the invocation of God may fill us for ever so that we may not corrupt it but, just as we were once made holy, so we may remain so for all eternity. Let us understand how holy thy Name is, that is, it is holy in all things and when we remember such holiness we should be afraid to sin. If anyone is a good Christian he does good work, so that in this way the name of Christ is hallowed in his servants; we pray that the name of God may be made holy by being praised and glorified in all our works. For whatever we do that is good is for his praise but whatever we do that is bad brings scorn upon him.[25]

Such a 'hallowing' of those who pray is therefore a hallowing of all creation, by returning everything made to a right relationship with its creator. Such a redeeming work must be constantly worked for but it is a gift of God which must also be asked for:

> Make us such, Father, that we may deserve to understand and grasp how great your hallowing is . . . that you may appear as hallowed in our hallowed way of life.[26]

Thy kingdom come

The next clause also relates to heaven, and is a prayer that the kingdom of God will come, which is seen as both a prayer for the indwelling of heaven in each soul now but also as a prayer of longing for the total rule of Christ on earth:

> Desire the heavens to be now and within us. Christ reigns daily in those who pray when the rule of the devil has been cast out of their hearts and God has begun to hold sway.[27]

But this also raises the question of unanswered prayer, since the kingdom does not seem to have come however often it is prayed for. In a sense there is no such thing as unanswered prayer; the dimension of time is not the same as the eternity of God, where all prayer is granted; on earth, the answer is always 'yes' but not always in the way expected or at the time it is asked:

> It also sometimes happens that we seek things entirely related to salvation with our eager petitions and right actions and yet we do not immediately obtain what we ask. The result of our petitions is postponed to some future time, as when

we daily ask the Father on bended knees, saying, 'Thy kingdom come'; we are not going to receive the kingdom as soon as our prayer is finished but at the proper time.[28]

Though this is true, in another sense the 'kingdom' is seen as already being given to those who ask for it:

What is the kingdom of God? Eternal blessedness, as it is said, 'Come, ye blessed of my Father' (Matthew 15.34). The almighty God reigns in his chosen ones by faith, hope and love and all good works; the devil reigns in us by greed, drunkenness, hatred and all evils; so we pray that it may be the Lord who reigns in us by righteousness and not the devil by sin.[29]

The journey of prayer towards the Father in heaven is life-long, but it may contain times when the peace of the kingdom is experienced as a present reality:

We are making a sea-voyage and are still on the journey. But there are times when we are wearied with travelling and the Lord grants tranquillity to our senses and quiet to our souls; this prayer of quiet is a foretaste of the kingdom for which we pray continually.[30]

Thy will be done on earth as it is in heaven

The next clause, that the will of God may be done on earth as it is already done in heaven, is a reminder that the angels, who always behold the face of God, perfectly do his will; but also that, for mankind, the will of God is summed up in the word 'redemption':

The will of God is the salvation of all . . . in other words, we are saying, 'Father, just as those in heaven are saved by knowing you, so also are those who are on earth'.[31]

It is also a reminder that the will of God is not to be confused with the will of the person praying, for, however clear it is to the petitioners that what they ask is right, there is no guarantee that this is so:

> We are admonished to include in the Lord's Prayer, 'Thy will be done', that is, not our own. For if we remember as well that saying of the apostle, 'We do not know what to pray for as we ought' (Romans 8.26), we shall understand that sometimes we beg for things opposed to our salvation and are very appropriately denied these things that we ask for earnestly by him who knows what is right for us more truly than we do.[32]

The will of God is being done on earth by continual prayer for the indwelling of Christ:

> In heaven the angels who never sinned do your will and their service is always acceptable to you; so let your good will be done on earth so that your servants may be pleasing to you. By heaven we understand the Lord Jesus Christ, by earth, the church. We know that as a man is to a woman, so is heaven to earth. From heaven the church receives all its fruitfulness, 'every good and perfect gift cometh from above' (James 1.17). Just as your will is done in heaven, which is Christ, so may it be done in the church, which is his body. As it is done in the heaven of just men, so may it be done also in the earth of sinners by their repentance.[33]

Give us this day our daily bread

The next clause links heaven and earth, the petitions connected with heaven to those concerned with earthly matters. This link is Christ, seen as the bread of life, which is love:

> Give us this bread as long as we live on earth . . . we beg you to give it us today because unless we receive it in this life, we shall not be ready to receive it in the life to come.[34]

45

Though one meaning of the 'bread' must be the 'eucharistic bread', another and equally valid meaning, and one emphasized in the early Church, was that it meant the Scriptures, which were broken open when they were read:

> By breaking the bread which he gave to his disciples, the Lord designates the opening of the secret meanings by which the world was to be nourished unto perpetual salvation. We cannot ourselves penetrate to the inner meaning of the bread of life but true understanding of it will be opened to us by him.[35]

To ask for this bread of love is always to receive it:

> We must not fear that, if we seek the gift of love from the Lord with deep devotion and say from the depth of our hearts, 'Give us today our daily bread', he will let our hearts be narrowed into the rigidity of hatred.[36]

This daily bread has also a natural meaning and includes what is needed to sustain earthly life, as well as being a request with a deeper meaning:

> Give us this day our daily bread: bread means all that is necessary for us in food, drink, clothing, to be given us today in this temporal life. By daily bread we can understand the body and blood of Christ of which he said, 'Unless you eat of this bread' (John 6.54). Let us pray that in receiving his body and his blood, by that which we see with our eyes we may receive that which we do not see, that is, almighty God: 'whoso eateth my flesh and drinketh my blood remains in me and I in him' (John 6.51). Where it says 'daily', perhaps we think we cannot be referring to the reception of communion, since there are those who think they cannot receive it daily because of sin. There are others, however, who do so, remembering that the Lord said to Zacchaeus, 'Today I must stay in your house', and he received him joyfully (Luke 19.5). Those who feel they cannot do this are

saying with the centurion 'Lord, I am not worthy to receive you under my roof' (Matthew 8:5) and they are adding by implication, 'I will come another day'. But Augustine says of this kind of humility, 'Brothers, I am pleased with your humility in fearing to receive the body and blood of the Lord, but it would be better if you were to receive it as cleansing for your sins and as repentance'. By bread we also understand the word of God speaking in the law, the prophets, the Psalms and the Gospels. In the time of our mortal life, refresh us with the teaching of the holy Scriptures, so that, as our body is refreshed by earthly food, so this spiritual food may refresh our souls to love and knowledge of you.[37]

The prayer for bread is to be offered daily, until life opens out into the great and ultimate day of the Lord:

He who today prays to God, who is from infinity to infinity, not only for this day but for each day, will be ready to receive from him even greater things.[38]

And forgive us our trespasses, as we forgive those who trespass against us

In this section of the prayer, repentance and sorrow for sin predominate. The severe note of reality reminds us that those who do not forgive cannot themselves be forgiven, not because of any arbitrary refusal by God, but because only by forgiving can the heart be ready to receive forgiveness:

If we want to be judged mercifully we must ourselves be merciful to those who have offended us, for we shall be forgiven to the degree that we have forgiven those who have injured us by any wrongdoing whatsoever.[39]

Such forgiveness is always necessary, even for those who have been baptized:

Whoever has been cleansed in the baptismal font and has received pardon for sins has no need to be cleansed again, and, moreover, cannot be cleansed again in the same way. It is necessary only to have the daily defilements of worldly life wiped away by the daily forgiveness of the Redeemer. The whole body together with its actions is clean, with the exception only of those things that cling to the mind because of temporal cares. It is for cleansing from daily defilement that we say daily in prayer, 'forgive us our trespasses as we forgive those who trespass against us'.[40]

It is not only by doing wrong actions that the soul is blinded by sin; it is also by failing to do good:

We are debtors to God in two ways, either by doing what he has forbidden or by not doing what he has commanded. Do we love God and our neighbour as he commanded? We are debtors, sinners. Do we honour our parents? We are debtors and sinners. Do not kill, do not commit adultery, do not swear, do not give false witness: we are daily offending against what he has commanded and so we are his debtors. If we would be forgiven by the Lord we must forgive others from the heart; or else we are doubly disobedient both by our own sins and by not loving our neighbour as we are commanded, since we do not forgive. He who taught us to pray about our offences and sins promised that his fatherly mercy and pardon would follow us . . . In this life he forgives our daily and individual sins, without which we cannot live in this life (1 John 1.7).[41]

There is here an awareness of the dialectic of being and becoming; the death and resurrection of Christ have redeemed mankind in one cosmic event, but each person had still to appropriate freely that fact into himself, and this is therefore a continual request:

The blood of Jesus his Son cleanses us from all sins. For the sacrament of the Lord's passion has equally freed us from all sin in baptism and the grace of our Redeemer forgives whatever we have committed through daily frailty after baptism. With humility we daily confess our errors to him when we receive the sacrament of his blood. After forgiving those who trespass against us, we entreat that our trespasses be forgiven us, praying that, mindful of his passion, we may gladly bear all adversities.[42]

Loving-kindness, good intentions, forgetting rather than forgiving, are never enough; the forgiveness that is being sought here is a deeper aspect of the fire of charity, which is God, and which includes truth as well as love:

> Charity covers a multitude of sins, especially when someone says truthfully to God, 'forgive us our trespasses as we forgive those who trespass against us'. And indeed all good works that we profess wipe away and cover the faults we commit, but this is said particularly about the charity by which we give to our neighbours those things that were given to us, because it is just in the sight of God that it be measured out to us according to the measure of devotion that we have ourselves measured.[43]

It is necessary, therefore, to be able to realize that salvation is dependent not just on interior and personal sorrow but upon the practical matter of the attitude each has towards others:

> O Almighty God, just as we forgive those who have sinned against us, do you forgive us. If we have not forgiven them, do not forgive our sins against you, as it is said, 'if you do not forgive, neither will my Father forgive you your sins' (Matthew 7.15).[44]

And lead us not into temptation

This is a clause about self-knowledge, as well as one that affirms the place of humility in life. Temptations are seen as having a positive role in life, enabling clarity and understanding of the

self in all its weakness and showing to what depths it is capable
of falling:

> The gifts our soul has received are unknown to everyone
> except God. They are unknown even to ourselves. Through
> temptations, they become known. Thereafter we cannot be
> ignorant of what we are, for we know ourselves . . . and we
> look to the future and prepare ourselves against what may
> befall us.[45]

But, aware of the weakness within, that God allows to continue
out of his infinite respect for freedom, we also need to ask that
such knowledge may not be too much to be borne:

> Do not allow us to be tried by the devil beyond our capacity,
> but with the trial also 'provide a way by which we may
> endure' (1 Corinthians 10.13).[46]

Temptation can be seen as the spurious attraction of evil for
weakness, and, because of this meaning of 'temptation', it is
proper to ask that it may not be too overwhelming to resist. But
'temptation' can also be seen as something allowed by God,
who does not override free will; in which case such testing can
be seen as a chance to increase in strength of commitment to
Christ. The way of growing up to the full measure of maturity in
Christ is not an easy gift of God given once for all but a vital
part of existence:

> There is one kind of temptation that is a testing, as God
> tempted Abraham to prove his faith; there is another tempta-
> tion that is of the devil, for 'God tempts no one' (James
> 1.13). We pray not to be led into the devil's temptation
> beyond what our frailty is able to bear. God is said to lead us
> into temptation when he does not free us from temptation.[47]

But deliver us from evil

The prayer for delivery out of all evil is most earnestly commented on, since in life there is always the possibility of failure. Its seriousness is underlined by commentators who illuminate it by using the imagery of battles, of soldiers, of fighting, which has been used in this connection from the first century to today:

> The soldiers of Christ – namely those who are learning contemplation and practising prayer – are always ready for the hour of conflict. They are never very much afraid of their open enemies, for they know who they are and are sure that they cannot prevail against the strength given them by the Lord . . . Those whom they fear and fear rightly, and from whom they always ask the Lord to deliver them, are enemies who are treacherous, devils who transform themselves and visit them disguised as angels of light.[48]

There is no permanent deliverance from the condition of being human during life on earth, and so this prayer continues to be needed:

> The whole life of man on earth is temptation. Let us pray to be delivered from temptation, not that we should not be tempted, which is impossible for those on earth, but that we may not yield when we are tempted.[49]

Amen

This word contains echoes of the earliest forms of Christian liturgy, when all the congregation, according to third-century writers, united in the great 'amen' at the end of the central prayer of the eucharist: 'So be it is said to signify and confirm this prayer. "For thine is the kingdom and the power and the glory for ever and ever."'

It is a final affirmation that whatever has been said was truly meant:

'Amen' is the seal set on this prayer, like a seal that confirms a legal document. It is as if those who say this more especially confirm that last clause, saying, 'Indeed, what I have said I meant. If I have forgiven those who have sinned against me, forgive me whatever I have done against you; but if I have not forgiven, neither should you forgive me.'[50]

Conclusion

These comments on the Our Father are based on the premise that it is a prayer that at once links those praying into the relationship of Christ to the Father, and, since it is plural, with all others, as children of God; they therefore become part of the eternal love between Father and Son, which is the Holy Spirit. This sonship is not remote; it is not a matter of undertaking severe training to attain prayer at the end of a hard road. It is given at once, in the present tense, now and available for use. It is prayer that already exists and can be entered into. It is for all – for Tatiana and Ambrose, a married and elderly couple in the church of the martyrs; for the new monks of Gaul, converted barbarians who wanted their lives to be based on the traditions of the desert monks of Egypt; for the energetic but unlearned new Christians of Anglo-Saxon England; for a small group of middle-class young ladies of northern Spain, who were becoming nuns just when the Reformation was happening in Northern Europe. These were not theologians or academics, or specially educated – just people baptized and serious about a life of prayer. The Our Father is available for all, while it is not separate from the doctrines of creation, redemption and sanctification.

The shape of the Paternoster is consistent with all prayer. It has two parts: the first begins in heaven and is linked to the second, earthly needs, by bread, which is Christ, who is love. The Our Father gives the outline and pattern for all prayer, and the more it is repeated the more it becomes physically part of those who use it, by being contained in the memory; and therefore the more it is absorbed, the more the commandment is fulfilled to 'pray without ceasing' (1 Thessalonians 5.17). It can continue as prayer silently contained within the heart, so that the Christian who is among other people is always saying for them with Christ, 'Our Father'.

Basic as it is to Christianity, nevertheless the Our Father is not a ritual formula that can produce a result, nor is it a prayer that has to be used. Each author cited sees it, not as a limiting straitjacket, but as a working pattern by which Christians enter into prayer in the Spirit, which is the dynamic life of love in the Trinity. It provides a guaranteed way into the life of God, but God is always larger than his own rules. To underline this I will end with a quotation from Tolstoy's story, 'The Three Old Men'. He describes three very old men who had lived on a remote island, unknown all their lives. They received a visit from an archbishop, who asked them how they prayed; they told him that all they ever said was: 'You are three and we are three; have mercy on us.'

Slightly scandalized, the archbishop patiently taught them, word by word, the scriptural prayer of the Our Father, and left them saying it. But in the night, as his ship sailed away, he saw a light following the ship:

He saw the three old men running on the sea, their grey beards showing dazzlingly white, their feet overhauling the ship as though it had been standing still.

When the old men reached the ship they raised their heads above the side and said they had forgotten the Lord's Prayer and asked to be taught it again.

But the archbishop said: 'Your prayer too, O ancient men of God, was profitable unto the Lord. It is not for me to teach you. Pray you rather for us sinners.' And the archbishop bowed to his feet before the old men. For a moment they stood motionless – then turned and went back across the sea and until morning a light could be seen glowing in the direction in which they had departed.[51]

Notes

1 Origen, *On Prayer*, ch. 2.(hereafter 'Origen'). (Translations of ancient sources throughout this chapter are my own.)
2 Origen, ch. 18 .
3 Origen, ch. 33.
4 John Cassian, *Conferences*, Conference 9: 'Abba Isaac On Prayer', 18.2 (hereafter 'Cassian').
5 Cassian, 25.1.
6 Bede, *Commentary on Luke*, in *Bedae Venerabilis Opera*, CCSL CXX, ed. D. Hurst (Turnholt, Brepols, 1960), pp. 229–230.
7 Bede, *Commentary on Samuel*, in *Bedae Venerabilis Opera*, CCSL CXIX, ed. D. Hurst (Turnholt, Brepols, 1969), p. 87.
8 Bede, *Samuel*, pp. 815–24.
9 Bede, *Luke*, p. 227.
10 Bede, *Luke*, p. 227.
11 *Rule of St Benedict*, ch. 13.
12 Bede, 'Letter to Egbert'.
13 Anglo-Saxon Our Father, Worcester, *c.* 1000, Oxford Bodleian Library Ms Junius 121, fol. 43 (alternative version in *Anglo-Saxon Poetry*, tr. S. A. J. Bradley, Everyman's Library, London, Dent, 1982).
14 Alfred the Great, his preface to his translation of Gregory the Great's *Pastoral Care.*
15 Alcuin, *Liber de Divinis Officiis*, *PL* 101:1265Ff. (hereafter 'Alcuin').
16 Teresa of Avila, *The Way of Perfection*, ch. xxvii–xlii (hereafter 'Teresa').
17 For a similar approach, cf. Anthony Bloom, 'Living Prayer', in *The Essence of Prayer* (Darton, Longman & Todd, 1986), pp. 18–19.
18 Teresa, ch. xxxvii.
19 Cassian, xviii.2.
20 Bede, *Commentaries on the Catholic Epistles*, in *Bedae Venerabilis Opera*, CCSL CXXI, ed. D. Hurst (Turnholt, Brepols, 1962), 1 Peter 1.17, p. 75.
21 Teresa, ch. xxvii.
22 Cassian, xx.11.
23 Teresa, ch. xxviii.
24 Cassian, xviii.5.
25 Alcuin, col. 1266B.
26 Cassian, viii.5.
27 Origen, ch. 25.
28 Bede, *Homilies*, 'Sermon after Easter' 11.12, in *Bedae Venerabilis Opera Homiletica*, CCSL CXXII, ed. D. Hurst (Turnholt, Brepols, 1955), p. 261 (hereafter '*Homilies*').

29 Alcuin, col. 1266D.
30 Teresa, ch. xxx.
31 Cassian, xx.2.
32 Bede, *Homilies*, 'Sermon at the Greater Litanies', 2.14, p. 277.
33 Alcuin, cols. 1266D–1267A.
34 Cassian, 21.2.
35 Bede, *Commentary on Mark*, in *Bedae Venerabilis Opera*, CCSL CXXII, ed. D. Hurst (Turnholt, Brepols, 1955), p. 529.
36 Bede, *Homilies*, 'Sermon at the Greater Litanies', 11.14, p. 131.
37 Alcuin, cols 1267C–1268B.
38 Origen, ch. 27.16.
39 Cassian, xxii.2.
40 Bede, *Homilies*, 'Homily for Holy Thursday', 11.5, p. 217.
41 Alcuin, col. 1268D.
42 Bede, *Homilies*, 'Sermon at the Greater Litanies', 11.14, p. 273.
43 Bede, 'On the Catholic Epistles', in *Bedae Venerabilis Opera*, CCSL CXXI, ed. D. Hurst (Turnholt, Brepols, 1955), 1 Peter 4, p. 110.
44 Alcuin, col. 1268D.
45 Origen, ch. 29.17.
46 Cassian, xxiii.1.
47 Alcuin, col. 1267D.
48 Teresa, ch. xxxviii.
49 Origen, ch. 29.9.
50 Alcuin, col. 1269B.
51 Leo Tolstoy, 'The Three Hermits', in *Master and Man and Other Parables and Tales* (Everyman's Library; London, J. M. Dent & Sons; New York, E. P. Dutton & Co.), p. 180.

Sources in English Translation

Alfred the Great, Preface to his translation of Gregory's *Pastoral Care*, in *Alfred the Great*, tr. Simon Keynes and Michael Lapidge (Harmondsworth, Penguin Books, 1983).

Bede, *Homilies on the Gospels*, tr. L. Martin and D. Hurst, 2 vols (Cistercian Studies; Kalamazoo, MI, Cistercian Publications, 1991).

Bede, 'Letter to Egbert', in *Ecclesiastical History of the English People*, tr. J. McClure (Oxford, Oxford University Press, 2000).

Cassian, John, *Conferences*, tr. Boniface Ramsey (Ancient Christian Writers; New York, Paulist Press, 1997).

Origen, *On Prayer*, tr. John J. O'Meara (Ancient Christian Writers; New York, Newman Press, 1954).

Teresa of Avila, 'The Way of Perfection', in *The Complete Works of Saint Teresa of Jesus*, vol. 2, tr. E. Allison Peers (London, Sheed and Ward, 1949).

3

ON PRAYING
THE APOSTLES' CREED

DAVID MOSS

I believe in God the Father Almighty,
*   creator of heaven and earth*
And in Jesus Christ, His only Son, our
*   Lord, who was conceived by the*
*   Holy Spirit, born from the Virgin*
*   Mary, suffered under Pontius Pilate,*
*   was crucified, dead and buried,*
*   descended to hell, on the third day rose*
*   again from the dead, ascended to*
*   heaaven, sits at the right hand of God*
*   the Father almighty, thence He will*
*   come to judge the living and the dead;*
I believe in the Holy Spirit, the holy
*   Catholic Church, the communion of*
*   saints, the remission of sins, the*
*   resurrection of the flesh, and eternal*
*   life. Amen.*

As he climbed up to repeat the Creed they all shouted his name to one another in a clamorous outburst of thanksgiving – everyone who knew him, that is; and was there anyone present who did not? Then in more subdued tones the word passed from joyful mouth to joyful mouth among them all: 'Victorinus, Victorinus!' Spontaneous was their shout of delight as they saw him, and spontaneous their attentive silence to hear him. With magnificent confidence he proclaimed the true faith, and all the people longed to clasp him tenderly to their hearts. And so they did, by loving him and rejoicing with him, for those affections were like clasping hands.

This is the dramatic account that St Augustine offers us of Marius Victorinus' profession of faith in Book VIII. 2 of the *Confessions*. Victorinus himself had been, until an old man, a brilliant professor of rhetoric who had been honoured with a statue in the Roman Forum. However, in about 355 he converted to Christianity. Undoubtedly, the conversion of so important and educated a citizen of Rome profoundly influenced Augustine; more so in that Victorinus had been the translator of those very 'platonist books' (*libri platonicorum*) that had been so influential in his own conversion.[2] 'Rome stood amazed' at these events, wrote Augustine, with hyperbolic glee. And why? Because at the very moment at which Victorinus was to have made a private and altogether more seemly profession of faith for one so eminent, he was emboldened to abjure this arrangement, mount a raised platform in the church and recite the Creed from memory before the assembled congregation.

Augustine himself was not a direct witness to these dramatic events. Instead, the story was told to him by Simplicianus when Augustine himself was wavering over his own conversion. Thus, just as Victorinus' conversion opens Book VIII of the *Confessions*, so Augustine's own conversion closes it. And – as Augustine understands matters – just as Simplicianus had told him (Augustine) the story of Victorinus' conversion with the aim of 'inculcating in me that humility of Christ', so, we may suppose, he now hands on this account to his readers with the very same intent.

The creed that Victorinus proclaimed was not, of course, the Apostles' Creed. However, the context in which this dramatic and choreographed credal profession of faith occurred (the so-called 'rendering' of the creed),[3] and further its archetypical presence behind Simplicianus' own 'handing on' of the conversion of Victorinus to Augustine, is that dimension of the Creed I wish to explore in this chapter on praying the Apostles' Creed. For this context, I want to suggest, involves coming to understand 'credal' prayer as that graced receptivity to the *Faith-as-tradition* that paradoxically confronts us with an experience of *loneliness* residing at the origin of the Church of Christ. Thus, while the ancient rite of 'rendering' the creed dramatizes the dynamic of tradition as a handing over (*traditio*) and receiving, in the context of the baptismal liturgy with its plunge into the waters of Christ's death (Romans 6.3–4), more so does it dramatize the *origin* of that tradition that erupts from the Father's decision to hand over (*paradothenai*) the Son into the hands of sinful men (Luke 24.7). The tradition may comfort and console, but it does so through telling of an original loneliness and abandonment. It is this polysemic 'handing over' that the Apostles' Creed testifies to in an abbreviated and paradigmatic form, where the abbreviation concerns precisely what the Scriptures say at length; and the paradigm concerns precisely the pattern of the Christian doctrine of God as Trinity: Father, Son and Holy Spirit.

In this chapter, then I do not intend to offer a 'reading' of the Apostles' Creed after the style of many illustrious theologians.[4] My intention is neither the explication of its doctrines nor the excavation of its history; rather, I want to offer a reflection on what it may mean for one who has been baptized to pray the Apostles' Creed first and foremostly in companionship with his or her fellow Christians.

Credal prayer

There will be more to say about the history and legend of the Apostles' Creed in the next section of this chapter, but for the moment let us ask how we should approach the Christian creeds as *prayers*; as precisely those who pray these words in the context of the liturgies of the Eucharist or Baptism, in the Offices of Morning or Evening Prayer, or even in the context of personal prayer, if we were to take a creed as the basis for our meditation. How are we to say and pray these words?

Now by this question I do not intend to raise the idea of any sort of special spiritual technique. Christians do say and pray the creeds in the sincere conviction that prayer is more than the outward performance of an obligation in which we tell God things he already knows. And even if at times prayer seems to become the dull repetition of texts we have long since memorized but still struggle to comprehend, do we not sense that this hardest and most demanding of duties would yield the brightest of illuminations if we would but surrender to it with all our heart? And if this is true of our personal and whispered prayers flung from the midst of our daily struggles and desires, how much more of those credal doxologies to God's grandeur and glory? For these abbreviated accounts narrate the very saving deeds that are at the foundation of the Christian faith: God's activity as manifest in creation; in the salvation of the world wrought through the life, death and resurrection of Jesus Christ; and now present in and through the Spirit, who enlightens, guides and heals. But as the world grows old around us and the death-dealing of both the cosmos and the human heart imperils the very intelligibility of our hope, do we feel ever more that the Faith demands that we speak a language without having first mastered its grammar? Thus, it seems to me that there are two preliminary points that we should and indeed need to make as we take up the idea of praying the creeds.

The first is that we should recognize the importance of that determinative *liturgical context* in which the creeds are recited and prayed; and second, that we need to reflect, if only a little, upon the fact that even the 'heavenly idiom' of liturgy will secure for us no timelessly valid vantage point from which to annotate, by some sort of spiritual *gnosis*, a glossary of eternal truths. The creeds have a history (a tradition) and, as their translation and transformations demonstrate, that history has still not ended.

First, then, the creeds are most fundamentally a form of *liturgical prayer*, and, to make a rather obvious point (although the point was not immediately clear to Marius Victorinus), their proper 'performance' should be undertaken in church. Indeed, whatever else becomes clear to us from Augustine's retelling of the story of Victorinus, it is that he could make no claim to be a Christian apart from a public profession of faith in 'Christ's church'.[5]

Liturgical prayer in all its many forms is ecclesial prayer, that is, the Church's prayer. Thus, if prayer in its widest sense is an expression of *our* communion with God, in a conversation in which God's Word always takes the initiative, then in liturgical prayer the 'our' of this prayer is precisely those persons baptized in the name of the triune God: in short, the Church community. As the prayer of the Church, liturgical prayer is marked by an official dimension, and, through some process of authorization, is understood to possess a normative status in the public life of the Christian community. Thus, Augustine introduces Victorinus' 'profession of faith' with the remark: '*Custom decrees* that those who are approaching your grace in baptism make their profession in the presence of the *baptized community* of Rome.'[6] Moreover, and this is particularly marked in the liturgical location of the Apostles' Creed,[7] liturgical prayer acts as an external expression of the unity in which the Church shares through its one baptism into Christ. Liturgical, and thus 'common prayer', promotes an experience of unity and, to the extent that all prayer expresses dimensions of the relationship between Creator and creature, *just so* does the experience of public communal prayer evoke the multivalent nature of that unity with especial intensity and scope.

We should tread carefully here however, for mention of 'intensity' in the context of common prayer can, unless we are careful, signal an often unconscious sense that the primary purpose of liturgical prayer and credal confession is the genera-tion of what we are apt to call today 'group identity'. There are several threads bound up in this observation and we would do well to draw them out briefly. The first is quite simply this. Con-formity to an invariant text, which may operate as a fixed point amid so much passing liturgical fashion, is not the first priority of liturgical prayer – although it would be manifestly wrong to dismiss this dimension entirely from the historical dynamic involved in 'the making of the creeds'.[8] The issue is not that this is entirely wrong or an abandonment of the gospel, only that beyond this creaturely experience of consolidating *koinonia* (which is always a gift from God) lies that divine reality that infi-nitely transcends all forms of common rite, symbol or creed. In counterpoint to this, however, we should also say that, although God utterly transcends our earthly language and forms, the doctrines of the creeds are hardly thereby to be abandoned in search of a 'deeper' experience of unity and commonality. For sure, as Henri de Lubac sagely remarks, 'In the actual recitation of my creed, I am not making an act of faith by doing so'; however, as he goes on to explain:

> If then, the creed gives us, more or less developed, the essential *content* of the faith, the act of faith which the creed presupposes gives us its *form* – and the very terms in which the creed is formulated make clear that the content, without the form, would not be just empty theory but a lie. In short, I can say *credo in Deum* because I have said in the first place 'I believe in you, my God'.[9]

Secondly, the catholic tradition has always recognized that the affirmation of dogmatic truth, the truths secured and reiterated in the creeds, while not of itself constituting the *act of faith*, is none the less directionless and impoverished without such an objective expression. More so, such an abandonment of dogmatic expression would make the transcendence of God prey to what he signifies for me alone in the contingencies of my own life.

Finally, with regard to the intensity of Christian common life and worship, we cannot fail to wonder why, if liturgical prayer has so high a calling with regard to that gift of unity that is God's alone, we are forever tempted, in crass or sophisticated styles, to diffuse this binding of form and content in ecclesial prayer? And here I think we would do well – in humble recognition of the Church's context in a liberal modern society – not to jump unthinkingly into yet another wearisome round of the 'modernizers versus traditionalists' debate, but rather to begin to explore the manner in which the conditions of Church life and worship in modernity have increasingly determined that we carry our expectations of 'private' prayer into the experience of corporate liturgical prayer. There is perhaps increasing recognition of this fact among those charged with supervising the good health of the Church's liturgies. So long, however, as Christians schooled in the ways of the world participate in liturgical prayer with the expectation, conscious or unconscious, that the measure of this act is given in meeting the hunger of individual piety, then the rite will actually work against itself. We shall return to this point of common recitation later.

Above, I indicated that there were two preliminary points that we should at least register before proceeding. If the first of these concerned issues surrounding *praying* the creed as a liturgical prayer, then the second concerns the *creed* that we are to pray together. Obviously, while the two points are not disconnected, they should not be run together in peremptory fashion. Thus, if we may express some confusions today as to what we are doing when we pray the creeds together, so, I also suspect, we may wonder what is the meaning of these words that we are together confessing.

The great twentieth-century theologian Karl Rahner once wrote of the Apostles' Creed that, although it properly continues in use today as 'a permanent and binding norm of the faith', still it is hardly adequate to this task because it can no longer 'appeal directly to our contemporary intellectual and spiritual situation'.[10] It would be foolish to ignore Rahner's words and more so the evangelical passion they exhibit; but perhaps it would also be a little unwise *not* to ask whether the 'intellectual and spiritual situation' of Marius Victorinus was, for example, any more receptive to the gospel message than our situation today? Creeds, and no doubt especially creeds, can and have become a paradoxically privileged arena in which battles over fidelity to 'the Faith of our fathers' have been fought; the matter will, in a crucial sense, always be so.[11] Thus the persistent question today is: should we rewrite them so as to make them more understandable, acceptable and appropriable by this current generation? Again one can sense as many hackles rising here as impatient demands from liturgists convinced that our salvation rests in 'revision'. But this entire agenda, I want to suggest, is always in danger of abandoning that central spiritual reality – which first and foremostly demands of us prayer – with which creeds have to do: and that is, in the words of the Swiss theologian Hans Urs von Balthasar, the fact that 'the beginnings of tradition are in their innermost core traditionless, despite (or because of) the fact that God is handing himself on.'[12] This aphoristic and somewhat obscure remark is, I want to claim, a key to praying the Apostles' Creed in all its fullness and scope. But in order to explain this we must first retell something of the history of this very ancient Christian confession.

A symbol of faith

The legend of the Apostles' Creed is well known. We have it from early commentaries by St Ambrose and also Rufinus.[13] The story they have to tell, as no doubt they were told, is that on the threshold of the breaking up of the original apostolic band, and as each apostle prepared to take the Faith to the four corners of the known world, the Holy Spirit inspired each apostle in turn to contribute one of the twelve articles of the Apostles' Creed. The legend, however, although presenting us with a vital truth as to its provenance (to which we will return in a minute), obscures a rather more complicated history.

As J. N. D. Kelly reminds us in his scholarly and recondite study *Early Christian Creeds*, the baptismal liturgies, which undoubtedly provided the context for the earliest credal formulations, 'are jungle like in their complexity'.[14] Despite this we may bring some order to this complexity by suggesting a summary, although by no means strictly chronological, process. In the New Testament we clearly come across stereotypical confessions of faith that allowed the apostolic kerygma to be passed on orally in missionary preaching.[15] By and large these standard confessions are mainly christological, but in several places in the New Testament we can also find trinitarian or at least tripartite confessions of faith (notably, but not alone, in Matthew 28.19). These confessions, arising from different *Sitz im Leben*, none the less appear over time to grow together in the context of baptismal liturgy. Thus, in the writings of Tertullian, but most especially in the *Apostolic Tradition* of Hippolytus, we discover clear evidence of such a fusion as christological profession is bound into trinitarian structure in an *interrogatory* form.[16] In an interrogating, question-and-answer rite the candidate for baptism is asked to give assent to a confession of faith. Over time, it would appear that a plurality of local 'interrogatory' creeds of the second and third centuries migrated by the fourth century into a rather more stable and tripartate 'declaratory' form as a consequence of the Church's own catechetical needs and ministry. The Apostles' Creed as we now know it is believed to have emerged out of just such a process, and comes down to us as an expansion of an Old Roman baptismal creed known first from a letter of Marcellus of Ancyra to Pope Julius I in 340. A full text of the Apostles' Creed (known as the *textus receptus*), which probably originated in south Gaul, is found for the first time in an *Ordo Romanus* of 950.

Two things should be noted about this history and provenance. The first point is made by Edward Schillebeeckx when he writes of the *apostolic origin* of the Creed:

> Although the classic *symbolum* of faith was not formulated by the Apostles themselves, it may nonetheless correctly be called 'apostolic'. It is really a *regula* of the apostolic faith, and faithfully reflects the main themes of the apostolic *kerygma*, the apostolic catechesis of candidates for baptism, and the primitive christian confession of faith.[17]

The claim is of fundamental importance, for it tells us that in the Apostles' Creed we do indeed have access, via the witness of the apostles, to that very source of the tradition (the events and story of God-with-us) that they themselves handed over. Thus the Apostles' Creed, far from being one more doctrinal and deadening accretion upon a lively and sheerly existential faith, lets us *touch* (we could say) the traditionless source of the mystery of salvation: the new thing God has done in Jesus Christ (2 Corinthians 5.17). Moreover, and this is the second point, in that the creeds have their genesis in doxology, the Apostles' Creed (in particular) will be endangered by this charge of deadening – although never overrun by it – only to the extent that we exhaustively mistake its primary provocation for one of its tributary effects: that is to say, as a test for orthodoxy.[18]

The Apostles' Creed does not collate 'articles of belief', nor does it set before us a potted systematic theology. Indeed, while different creeds obviously stir different reactions in different people,[19] we should be alert to the fact that as a 'declaratory creed' the Apostles' Creed remains close to its catechetical context, and in this should not be compared too closely with, for example, a conciliar creed. The Apostles' Creed is a summary affirmation of the Christian story that the convert is invited to make his or her own in an act a confession before God that intimately involves the acts of acknowledgement and praise. Moreover, it is in this act of confessing the Creed that the meaning of its ancient title, the 'Symbol (*symbolum*) of Faith' becomes evident. Two interconnected realities are involved here, realities that we may see indicated in the theological history of two words – *confession* and *symbol* – in the context of the handing-on of tradition.[20]

The first – the act of *confession* – summons to mind the dynamism of the very act of faith itself as a stretching out and moving towards God. Indeed, its semantic history reveals how, in this one existential act, the different dimensions of recognizing one's own sinfulness, proclaiming God's mighty deeds and attesting the object of one's faith are all blended together. Together these elements fuse in an eminently personal act. As the story of the conversion of Marius Victorinus clearly indicates, however, this personal act is no individual or private affair. It is from the Church that I receive this Faith and it is within the Church that I believe and am bound to my brothers and sisters in Christ. Thus, it is precisely this communal aspect of the confession of faith that is expressed in the word 'symbol'. At the root of the theological appropriation of this Greek word, which was used in various different contexts, philosophic, religious and military alike, lies the sense of 'a sign of recognition' performed through the reconstitution of separated parts. Appearing first in the writing of St Cyprian when commenting upon a baptismal creed, the idea of the symbol was fairly rapidly adopted as naming a formula for that confession of faith that was normative for all Christians. As St Augustine writes: 'We call "symbol" the text which contains the faith ratified by our community, and the faithful Christian is recognized by this profession of it, as by the giving of a sign.'[21]

As Henri de Lubac has demonstrated (in practices hardly novel to Christian teachers down through the ages) all manner of further meanings have been given to the symbol of *the Symbol* in order to reveal its 'fitting' abbreviation of the Faith. Despite such allegoric effusion, however, de Lubac concludes his own profound examination of the Apostles' Creed with this trenchant remark: 'A personal and public commitment, the bond of communion with all other believers – that, then, is the two-fold reality signified and effected by the confession of faith in the recitation of the creed.'[22]

This may well seem to be a good place to conclude this chapter, most especially if we were to note that in the continuing history of this Creed it has remained in universal use in the West for baptismal services, survived the Reformation intact in all except one small detail (Luther substituted 'Christian' for 'Catholic') and in the last century was recognized as a rallying formulary for the ecumenical movement.[23] It can in this sense be seen to fulfil the requirements for being a true symbol of the Faith in practice and in promise. Indeed, when we use it, should we not justifiably feel that confidence and comfort of being bound into a universal declaration of apostolic faith – a true inheritance from the very origins of Christianity? The questioning that disturbs our reception of the Creed today, however, and to which I pointed in the first section of this chapter, remains and, I now want to suggest, may be taken up again from a final quotation from Henri de Lubac. He writes: 'The fact that we say the creed in the singular and in common is not without profound significance, and we must make sure we never lose sight of it.'[24] But what is this profound significance? And what must we never lose sight of?

In conclusion, I want to suggest that what this amounts to is most fundamentally a matter of *ecclesial* existence; and that it may be approached, in its deepest reaches, only through prayer and contemplation. What I am concerned about here has nothing to do with any fashion for liturgical revision but rather with drawing out the implication of our practice of praying these words in the conviction of our baptismal identity. For what is it that binds the 'I' of my confession to the 'you' of your self-same confession if not the 'handing over' (*traditio*) of the Son by the Father into the utter *aloneness* of abandonment and death, which I may come to recognize only through the pentecostal renewal of baptism? Praying the Apostles' Creed thus involves participation in this articulated and divine reality of love attested to in the tripartite structure of the Apostles' Creed. But it does so through no technique on our part – even if we must 'learn *to give back* our language, and our understanding, and ourselves' in this prayer.[25] This is what we must learn to do for sure (to hand on or over what we have received), but before this there is no learning to be done; much rather, if one can put it this way, there is only the onset of unlearning and of a vertiginous descent into loneliness. This, after all, is what the Apostles' Creed alludes to in its most expansive section. And something like this is that with which we have to do in the prayer of the Apostles' Creed: a 'having to do' that would wreck any fantasy we may entertain of a solitary and heroic 'knight of faith', for sure. In that *our* song-like profession of faith should approach that harmony whereby the dynamism of faith towards God instigates a unity of *convergence*, however, it does so only through participation in the death of the one who remains the loneliest person in the entire world – the unique one, Jesus Christ.[26] In other words, the unity we have, the unity of common confession, is first and foremost precisely not the unity of *our* common confession, but the unity won for us by the one who bore our sins of disunity even unto death.

Loneliness: at the origin of tradition

'Loneliness determines the moment of the Church's origin: and so for that reason it is also deeply stamped for her as the source of her community.'[27] This fine perception of Hans Urs von Balthasar is, I want to say, what the Creed witnesses to *as prayed* – as liturgical prayer. And to stand under it is to begin to sense with an ever-deepening discernment (*contemplation*) what this may mean for the community gathered here through its baptism into Christ's death.

We have spoken of the Apostles' Creed as an abbreviation of what the scriptural story tells us at length, and have discovered its provenance in the earliest layers of the baptismal traditions of the Church – indeed, in the very apostolic witness itself. But what lies at the origin of these traditions? For on the day of her birth the Church was without tradition. Certainly, we need to say immediately that the Church was not without 'precedent' in understanding its history (Hebrews 1.1); and indeed the scriptural hermeneutics of many of the Church Fathers is taken up with trying to understand, allegorically and symbolically, those clues in the story of creation and Israel that illuminate the story of salvation. But these clues remain indecipherable apart from the prevenient action of God who sends his only Son into the world so that all may be saved and have eternal life (Hebrews 9.12). For this there is no precedent, no tradition. This action on God's part is not the consequence of a 'history of effects' whereby God comes to learn what he must do next; nor, on our part, does it involve any extrapolation to Jesus Christ from the general drift of the story as a whole.

The Creed tells us something entirely different. It tells us first and foremost that to be baptized into Christ Jesus is to have one's entire life brought under the name and benediction of the triune God, Father, Son and Holy Spirit. Thus, this symbol of faith, composed as it is of its three core 'cells', is triune in structure in that it attests to the identity of God, who, in his essence (apart from creation, that is), is this inexhaustible relational process of love and surrender between the three 'persons' of the Trinity. The *unity* of the Trinity (a theme that has never been far from our reflections) is not that of consciousness or election but of kenotic, self-surrendering love. In trying to speak of this, we can no doubt mount only a rearguard action through pale analogy and metaphor before the mystery of God's life. But it is this *pattern* of love that the Creed labours to invoke: 'the original source of love that bestows itself infinitely ("Father")'; the 'self-declaration of love that receives and gives itself back infinitely ("Son")'; and that accord between giving and receiving that itself overflows 'into creation infinitely ("Spirit")'.[28] This abstraction, though, must not be misinterpreted, for it is, so the Christian faith claims, but one more (and still more severe) abbreviation of that reality we witness to in the life, death and resurrection of Jesus Christ. The divine character of love, lively and full of surprises in its selving and othering differentiations, now transcribed into the relentless (indicated in the Gospels through the little word *dei*, 'it is necessary') progress of Jesus towards his 'hour' – death on a cross.

Thus, if the form of the Apostles' Creed is trinitarian and demands that we find no other identification for God than through these 'communally authoritative [and] identity sustaining rules of discourse',[29] then this is only so as to render transparent the relation of the unity of God's life *in se* with the journey of the Son 'into the far country': in other words, the relation of the doctrines of the Trinity and incarnation. Can we therefore say that the hinge upon which the history of salvation hangs is the infinite 'handing over' of Father to Son and the Son's obedient giving back to Father in the Spirit, which, in the life of Jesus Christ and those who would follow his way, becomes precisely a *handing over into loneliness*?

On what grounds are we making these claims? We can give but a brief indication. Mary ('born of the Virgin Mary') is isolated by the message of the angel; she knows not how to respond to the angel, and it is only after the overshadowing of the Most High that she can be reintroduced into the community of family and tradition (Luke 1.28–29). Jesus is lost to his parents at the age of twelve, only to be discovered in the temple – alone amid the teachers (Luke 2.41–42). Thereafter, the momentum of loneliness gathers about this one. He is tempted alone (Matthew 4.1–2), he takes opportunities to be alone to pray (Matthew 14.23), and the loneliness of misunderstanding, suspicion and disbelief gathers about him even among those he has called to himself (Mark 10.35–36). All this, though, is but preparatory to the abandonment and loneliness of his end, where, in the disaster of his death and scattering of his disciples, he gathers to himself every sin, which means alienation from God and isolation from the triune life ('was crucified, died, and was buried'). We could extend this list by reading the unabbreviated scriptural story from the perspective of this ever-intensifying dynamic of aloneness. But to do so would simply be to compound with further evidence this one central fact. The more he is alone and lonely the more he is revealed as who he really is. His ever greater loneliness, to death and then beyond into the Easter Saturday of the silenced Word ('descended into hell') opens to us the raw, ever creative bond of his relationship to his Father ('The third day he rose again from the dead'). Thus von Balthasar is moved to conclude:

> The essence of the Church's community, which is more deeply socially bonded and rooted than any other earthly and fleshly community, flows out of the most extreme and exquisite loneliness imaginable, in which but one man, 'for the sake of the many', becomes the ultimate individual of all, utterly abandoned by God and man alike. *How could the birthmark of this origin not continually brand such a community!*[30]

This 'branding', to use a crass commercial analogy that has long since lost its torturous overtones, belongs to the Church in its credal formularies, its 'identity sustaining rules'; but these are not at its origin; they simply bear witness to this origin. And in this perhaps they scarcely comfort us in a way that we suppose our traditions should. This is the *difference* we must see if we are to pray the Apostles' Creed, but paradoxically it is a difference that can be contemplated only in prayer.

The community of the Church is born out of the loneliness of the cross. The community of the Church is community *in* this loneliness. It is precisely not the loneliness of a now far distant past that can be summoned by the imagination through the aid of tradition in order to facilitate a sympathy with the risk, heroism and sacrifice of this dying man. But how then are we to interpret this loneliness to which the Creed gives abbreviated testimony in its binding of form and content: a 'realized transcription' of divine unity into 'the conditions of our existence'?[31]

The question concerns not the common condition of human loneliness that we all experience. Indeed, many Christians no doubt often experience this loneliness in a Church that is no longer the one they once knew, just as others experience a lonely despair at the ineptitude, even autism, of a Church that fails to become that society of liberation it is called to be. But, once again, to interpret this loneliness as a true measure of the providence of God would be catastrophically to mistake myself for God.

This is not to say that needs and desires are unimportant to Christian discipleship or church life. No doubt many Christians, on the path towards true discipleship, have drunk deeply from the wells of their 'personality type' and the like. But to the extent that their paths are directed to God, so they have recognized that such 'differences of persons' are too important for them to be taken as a measure of the wisdom of God. Our healing cannot come from our own selves; rather are we dependent upon boundless resources of grace, which are always beyond our own manufacture. And here, at this point, the true nature of Christian solitude comes into focus. For Christian loneliness exists in this fact: that the Church in its origin exists as the assembly of a group of abandoned people *gathered* together about *the* Abandoned One (John 19.25–27).

Does this, though, not sound like a counsel for despair? More so for a retreat into an afflicted and fearful laager whose doors are firmly bolted to the outside world (John 20.19)? To understand that it is not is to begin to understand that the enigmatic logic of the loneliness of Christ in his plunge into the abandonment of death is but the revelation of his dependency on, and so unity with, his Father. His handing over into the hands of those who will ultimately destroy him – which, of course, is prefigured in his own handing of himself over into the elements of eucharistic *koinonia* (1 Corinthians 11.23–24) – points continually towards that mystery of divine life that is utterly creative. The Apostles' Creed retells the narrative that demonstrates to us finally and completely that, although 'self-preservation is massively destructive, self-expenditure is even more fulsomely creative';[32] and this because (and the Creed tells us this also), it describes the very manner of God's life. As such, we who would confess this Creed cannot do so apart from a falling towards this loneliness that is the Son's, and which is our convergence with one another in the Spirit of Christ.

Prayer is that which introduces us to this fathomless, providential mystery and that which haltingly, perhaps laboriously, sometimes wondrously, begins to let us see one another anew in Christ: not as parts of a collective, nor as participants in a common enterprise, but paradoxically as *sharing* this enigmatic gift of Christ's loneliness: a divine handing over that will become for us a tradition of faith. To pray the Apostles' Creed – a tradition that takes us back to the traditionless origin of testimony – is to contemplate the fact, as von Balthasar reminds us, 'that loneliness in the Church belongs to her essence'. We should recall that the fundamental *difference* that repeatedly reappears in 'classical Christian paradigms of meeting God through cognition and knowing him through love is the question of whether this new perception is to be seen as being essentially disruptive of other cognitions and affections or in continuity with them'.[33] The Apostles' Creed teaches us, above all, the mystery of the divine Trinity, a mystery that has turned the world upside down and has demanded of us a remaking of all our ideas of God and of ourselves. This disruption will never exhaust itself, just as we will never advance beyond its testimony. This divine Origin is witnessed to in faith every time I utter, with you, 'I believe in God . . .'.

Notes

1 The 'Textus Receptus', in J. N. D. Kelly, *Early Christian Creeds* (3rd edn, London, Longmans, 1972), p. 369.

2 Augustine, *Confessions*, tr. Maria Boulding OSB (London, Hodder & Stoughton, 1997),VII. 9. 13.

3 The 'rendering' of the creed (*redditio symboli*) was a rite that appears to have marked the 'culmination of the catechetical training leading up to the sacrament [of baptism]. At a certain stage in the training . . . the bishop formally "delivered" the creed (this was the *traditio symboli*) to the more advanced catechumens. It was then their business to learn and assimilate it, so as to be able to reproduce it as their own spiritual possession on the eve of their initiation. The theory was that the creed was a secret formula which could not be written down but must be memorized by the

faithful.' J. N. D. Kelly, *Early Christian Creeds* (London, Longman, 1972), p. 32.

4 For example: Karl Barth, *Dogmatics in Outline* (London, SCM Press,1988); Hans Urs von Balthasar, *Credo: Meditations on the Apostles' Creed* (Edinburgh, T. & T. Clark, 2000); Hans Küng, *Credo: The Apostles' Creed Explained for Today* (London, SCM Press, 1993); Nicholas Lash, *Believing Three Ways in One God: A Reading of the Apostles' Creed* (London, SCM Press, 1992); Wolfhart Pannenberg, *The Apostles' Creed: In the Light of Today's Questions* (London, SCM Press, 1972).

5 Augustine, *Confessions*, VIII. 2. 4.

6 Augustine, *Confessions*, VIII, 2. 5, my italics.

7 In the western Church, by the Middle Ages, the Apostles' Creed was everywhere employed at baptism. It has also appeared at different times and in different traditions in the daily Offices.

8 The phrase is Frances Young's in her *The Making of the Creeds* (London, SCM Press, 1992). See especially ch. 1.

9 Henri de Lubac, *Christian Faith: The Structure of the Apostles' Creed* (London, Geoffrey Chapman, 1986), p. 172.

10 Karl Rahner, *Foundations of Christian Faith* (London, Darton, Longman & Todd, 1978), p. 449.

11 Thus Stephen Sykes' important suggestion that 'Christianity is to be understood as an essentially contested concept'. See his argument developed in *The Identity of Christianity* (London, SPCK, 1984), pp. 251ff.

12 Hans Urs von Balthasar, *Explorations in Theology* IV: *Spirit and Institution* (San Francisco, CA, Ignatius Press, 1995), p. 265.

13 *The Explanatio Symboli ad Initiandos: A work of Saint Ambrose*, ed. and tr. Dom R. H. Connolly (Cambridge, Cambridge University Press, 1952), pp. 3, 4, 10, 11. *Rufinus: A Commentary on the Apostles' Creed*, tr. J. N. D. Kelly (London, Longmans, Green and Co., 1955), p. 2.

14 Kelly, *Early Christian Creeds*, p. 32.

15 In the sermons of Peter and Paul in the Acts of the Apostles we come across classical patterns for the handing over of the Faith that focus on stereotypical formulas concerning, centrally, the death, resurrection and ascension of Christ: Acts 2.14–39; 3.12–26; 4.9–12; 8.16–41; 10.34–43.

16 *The Apostolic Tradition of Hippolytus*, tr. B. S. Easton (Cambridge, Cambridge University Press, 1934), II. 21.

17 Edward Schillebeeckx, *Revelation and Theology* (London, Sheed & Ward, 1967), pp. 230–1.

18 In this sense Martin Luther's revision of the form of the Roman Mass in 1523, his *Formula Missae et Communionis*, designated the Nicene Creed 'a sacrifice of praise' (*sacrificium laudis*), and so recaptured (ironically, more correctly for the Apostles' Creed

than for the Nicene Creed) something of a creed's original purpose as a confession of faith: an expression of praise before the lordship of Jesus Christ.

19 One thinks of the perplexed reaction of contemporary Anglicans who, in fidelity to the rubrics of the *Book of Common Prayer*, are set to use the Athanasian Creed for thirteen days a year at Matins.

20 The following paragraph draws heavily on Henri de Lubac's fine concluding chapter to his *Christian Faith: The Structure of the Apostles' Creed*, entitled 'Faith and the profession of faith'.

21 Augustine, Sermon 214, 12, quoted in de Lubac, *Christian Faith*, p. 183.

22 de Lubac, *Christian Faith*, p. 188.

23 At the World Conference on Faith and Order in 1927 (Lausanne), representatives of churches from the East and West confessed the Apostles' Creed together and joined in the conviction that it was indeed a suitable statement of the Christian message.

24 de Lubac, *Christian Faith*, p. 188.

25 Lash, *Believing Three Ways*, p. 81.

26 The song-like character of the creeds is a recognition that recurs throughout the Christian tradition – 'the saving song of the creed', as Faustus of Riez calls the Apostles' Creed – and indeed the creeds have promoted many magnificent musical settings. This aspect of performing the creeds is highlighted with particular acuity by the Methodist theologian Geoffrey Wainwright in his important study *Doxology: The Praise of God in Worship, Doctrine and Life* (London, Epworth Press, 1980), ch. VI.

27 von Balthasar, *Explorations in Theology* IV, p. 275.

28 Küng, *Credo*, p. 9.

29 Lash, *Believing Three Ways*, p. 8.

30 von Balthasar, *Explorations in Theology* IV, p. 271.

31 Donald MacKinnon, 'The Relation of the Doctrines of the Incarnation and the Trinity' in Richard McKinney (ed.) *Creation, Christ and Culture* (Edinburgh, T. & T. Clark, 1976), p. 104.

32 Alan E. Lewis, *Between Cross and Resurrection: A Theology of Holy Saturday* (Grand Rapids, Eerdmans Publishing Co., 2001), p. 305.

33 Oliver Davis, *A Theology of Compassion* (London, SCM Press, 2001), p. 157.

4

HAIL MARY

SANTHA BHATTACHARJI

Hail Mary, full of grace, the Lord is with thee;
blessed art thou among women,
and blessed is the fruit of thy womb, Jesus.
Holy Mary, Mother of God,
pray for us sinners, now
and at the hour of our death. Amen.

The Hail Mary is one of the most used prayers in the Western Christian tradition, from at least the twelfth century until the present.[1] In modern times it is popularly associated with specifically Roman Catholic practices such as the rosary and the Angelus, which did not take on their modern form until the sixteenth century.

This chapter will concentrate on the use of the Hail Mary in the late medieval period, which forms the common tradition out of which most contemporary Western Christian denominations arose. This will allow us to explore the principles which gave rise to the extensive use of this prayer, and which made it, in medieval usage, one of the three basic prayers (along with the Our Father and the Creed) that all Christians were required to know.[2]

Why was the Hail Mary considered so fundamental? This chapter will argue that, contrary to what one might expect, it was not used primarily to draw attention to Mary as a separate focus of devotion apart from God. Rather, the prayer functions as an accessible point of entry into the whole doctrine of Christ's incarnation and redemption, doctrines that are in themselves somewhat abstract and paradoxical, and thus difficult to grasp.

In particular, we see devotions addressed to Mary developing during the late Middle Ages hand in hand with a greater
focus on the humanity of Christ. This fresh preoccupation
with the full humanity of Christ, with all its implications in
terms of his physical and emotional suffering, arose in
reaction to the emphasis of the early Middle Ages on Christ's
divinity. Necessarily, the Church's task in the early centuries
was to help people to perceive the victory of God through the
veil of Christ's apparent total defeat on the cross. We see this
early emphasis, for example, in the sixth century Passiontide
hymns by Venantius Fortunatus, where Good Friday is
described as a battle in which Christ is the triumphant victor.[3]
The result, however, was perhaps to lose sight of Christ as
suffering all the physical pains and limitations of human life;
to lose sight of the full human cost of the incarnation and
redemption. In one sense, therefore, medieval devotions to
Mary represent a prolonged meditation on the person and
role of Jesus himself.

In its earliest form, the Hail Mary consists of two scriptural
phrases, taken from different parts of the Gospel, and joined
together. The first is Gabriel's greeting to Mary at the Annunciation (Luke 1.28): 'Hail, thou that art full of grace, the Lord
is with thee'; the second is Elizabeth's greeting to Mary at the
Visitation (Luke 1.42): 'Blessed art thou among women and
blessed is the fruit of thy womb.' The putting together of these
two phrases of Scripture appears to go back to at least the
sixth century,[4] when they are found in a Coptic fragment. In
this version, 'blessed is the fruit of thy womb' is followed by
the words 'because thou didst conceive Christ, the Son of
God, the Redeemer of our souls'.[5] Their most obvious early
use, with a similar ending, is in the Eastern Orthodox liturgy,
in an invocation to the Mother of God that occurs after the
Consecration but before the Communion.[6] We then find
these two scriptural phrases, without any additional ending,
entering Western liturgy in the early eleventh century, as the
invitatory antiphon at the beginning of Matins on the fourth
Sunday of Advent, that is, the Sunday immediately before
Christmas.[7]

This liturgical origin helps to account for the strictly scriptural content of the prayer at this point. The Western medieval liturgy, for all its richness and variety, drew much of its material purely from the Bible; around the core texts of the Psalms and the Gospels it constructed a tissue of quotations from all parts of Scripture, only the hymns and collects being more derivative compositions. The effect of this restriction to Scripture is to tie a formal address to Mary closely to the moment of the Annunciation, which, in Christian tradition, is seen as the beginning-point of salvation. In other words, the piece of Scripture chosen as a way of focussing on Mary is just as much, if not more, about the saving activity of her Son.

This strictly scriptural version seems to have been the form in which the Hail Mary circulated in the twelfth century. Its growing importance is reflected in the commentary written on it before 1180 by Baldwin of Ford, later Archbishop of Canterbury.[8] This is also the time when it figures prominently in several collections of Miracles of the Virgin, although embedded in a great deal of more elaborate material addressed to her.[9] The fact that the recitation of this prayer by ordinary lay people is shown to secure the Virgin's compassionate aid demonstrates that it is already moving outside the bounds of the liturgy and becoming a popular private devotion.

On to this bare scriptural formula Pope Urban IV, in around 1263, is reputed to have added the name 'Jesus'.[10] This served to tie the prayer firmly into the other great medieval devotion of the time, the invocation of the name of Jesus. It may seem surprising to us now to realize that before the twelfth century relatively little attention was paid to Christ's earthly name. In the early centuries, the preferred terms were 'Christ', 'the Lord', 'the Son of God', all terms serving to emphasize his mission and his divine nature. Early Christians were fully aware that 'Jesus' was an ordinary Jewish name, being a form of 'Joshua', and therefore borne by many other Jews. For example, Gregory I, in his *Homily* on the Gospel for Easter Day, explains the words of the angel to the women at the tomb as follows: the angel is obliged to say, in careful detail, 'You seek Jesus of Nazareth, who was crucified', because otherwise the women would not be sure that he was speaking about the right 'Jesus'.[11]

A turning-point seems to come in the twelfth century in a text by Anselm of Canterbury, where he exploits the actual meaning of the name Jesus – God-is-salvation – to make a fervent prayer to Christ for deliverance from the judgement of God.[12] From that beginning, devotion to the Holy Name seems to have developed like wildfire. It was seen to embody in one word the whole doctrine of the incarnation (God becoming fully man) and redemption (God himself rescuing man from the consequences of his sinfulness). By adding the word 'Jesus' to the end of 'blessed is the fruit of thy womb', the Hail Mary took on a similar completeness. Not only does it now refer to the moment of incarnation, but it looks forward to what will be accomplished in Jesus, that is, his earthly ministry of teaching and healing, as well as his death on the cross and his resurrection. That the word 'Jesus' is a distinct addition to the prayers is borne out by the fact that Baldwin's commentary on the earlier version, while necessarily discussing what the blessed fruit of Mary's womb might be, nowhere uses the name Jesus, but instead refers to Christ, the seed of Abraham, the rod of Jesse, and similar Old Testament terms.[13]

It is in these two forms (the two scriptural phrases either with or without the addition of the name Jesus) that the Hail Mary was enjoined on the faithful as one of the three prayers that all Christians ought to know.[14]

Now let us look at how the Hail Mary, in these two forms, chiefly circulated in the fourteenth and fifteenth centuries. Here, the liturgy maintains its influence through an important bridge between public worship and private devotion: the Little Office of Our Lady.

This 'Little Office', in which the Hail Mary figured prominently (sometimes as an antiphon, more usually as a versicle and response), reflected the desire of the laity to participate in the ongoing, daily worship of the Church, but in a more manageable form.

Medieval devotion to the Virgin Mary, in the Christian West, arguably begins with the development of a set of Offices addressed to her. In the early Middle Ages, the canonical Office, the sequence of daily services other than the Eucharist, gradually took shape, falling into slightly different forms among the monastics on the one side and the secular clergy on the other. Both forms, however, shared the same basic sequence: Matins (the heaviest Office), Lauds, Prime, Terce, Sext, None, Vespers and Compline. Within each Office, the actual texts might vary between the different traditions, and the number of psalms recited might alter, but in both cases, the recitation of the Office, which was obligatory for monastics and clergy, represented a substantial daily task, one too heavy for the laity to fit into their daily lives. From the monastic point of view, however, the obligation was relatively light, and a tendency developed to attach a lot of extra prayers to the end of each Office, such as commemorations of benefactors, devotions to patron saints and prayers for the dead.

A complete Office of Our Lady, which also became obligatory, was the major medieval addition to the canonical Office, developing from around the eleventh century on; indeed, the earliest manuscripts of this Office are English.[15] There were three forms of the Office of Our Lady during the Middle Ages: the *officium plenum*, or full Office, which was said on feast days of Mary (such as the Annunciation, Purification or Nativity of Mary) in place of the canonical Office; the Little Office in choir, which was added on to the canonical Office on a daily basis; and the Little Office said out of choir. These gradations represent a progressive simplification.

The *officium plenum* had all the richness of any feast-day Office, with a wealth of antiphons, hymns and readings appropriate to the particular feast. It represented the actual canonical Office for that day. Much of the material was adapted from the Old Testament prophecies applied to the Virgin, the Song of Songs and the wedding psalms (e.g. Psalm 44 in the Vulgate, 45 in the Authorized Version), and this gave the Office of Our Lady a distinctively poetic, sensuous, romantic flavour, a kind of holiday atmosphere, compared to all the other Offices, whose material was drawn from other, more sober or more challenging parts of Scripture.[16] An example might be (from the feast of the Purification):

> Adorna thalamum tuum Syon, et suscipe
> Regem Christum. Quem virgo concepit, virgo
> peperit, et post partum quem genuit
> adoravit.

> Adorn your bridal chamber, O Syon, and
> receive Christ the King, whom a virgin
> conceived, a virgin bore, and, after giving
> birth, adored the one she had borne.[17]

This *officium plenum* was said in a slightly plainer form, suitable for a feria (i.e. an ordinary day), on Saturdays . The practice of dedicating Saturdays to Our Lady was initiated by Pope Urban II in 1095. His purpose, perhaps unfortunately to modern eyes, was to implore Mary's support for the First Crusade.[18] However, it is not this official purpose, soon forgotten, that kept these prayers in fervent use. Rather, as we are exploring here, it is to do with their innate attractiveness. Thus Saturday, which in liturgical use kept its Hebrew name of Sabbath (*in die sabbato*) was an appropriate day for the sense of holiday, lightness and rest conveyed by the Office of Our Lady, as well, of course, as leading into the most important day of the Christian week, Sunday.

In the *officium parvum*, the Little Office which was tacked on to the canonical Office on all the other days of the week, we find the same exotic texts, but in a briefer form. This was a 'Little' Office because of the drastically reduced form of Matins. In the canonical Office, Matins could have up to twelve psalms and include lengthy readings from the Church Fathers, such as Augustine, Leo and Bede; in the Little Office, there were only three psalms, and the 'readings' consisted of short invocations to Mary, often marked by rhyme and metre. An example might be:

Sancta maria,
piarum piissima,
intercede pro nobis,
sanctorum sanctissima:
ut per te, virgo,
nostra sumat precamina
qui pro nobis natus
regnat super aethera,
ut sua charitate
nostra deleantur peccamina.

(Holy Mary, most merciful of the merciful,
intercede for us, O holiest of the holy: that
through thee, Virgin, he may receive our prayers,
who, born for us, reigns above the skies, that by
his love our sins may be effaced.)[19]

Since the rhyme scheme was often a simple a-b-a-b pattern and the metre of the tumty-tum variety, this gave the whole Office a kind of childlike simplicity and innocence, which may eventually have recommended it to the laity as something easy to recite and understand. A further simplification in the Office of Our Lady is that it had only a few variations according to the liturgical season, instead of the complicated daily variations of the canonical Office.

This led naturally to the next step: the Little Office of Our Lady said not in church but privately, which was completely invariable and thus easy to master. It is this invariable Office that is found in the many surviving medieval Books of Hours. To produce an invariable text, each locality made its own selection from the seasonal variants, thus producing distinctive 'local rites', which help modern scholars to localize these prayer-books. A further important step was the translation of these Latin Books of Hours into the vernacular languages of Europe. In England we have a fifteenth-century Primer that gives us one of the earliest written forms of the Hail Mary in English.[20]

In spite of the rhymed invocations to Mary that take the place of Matins readings, and antiphons that also address her, the Little Office of Our Lady retains its emphasis on the incarnation of Christ. Reciting this Office was thus rather like celebrating Christmas every day. If we could imagine a modern spiritual practice based on the daily singing of Christmas carols, we could get some idea of why this Little Office proved so popular among the laity. In addition, the passion of Christ was not forgotten, as it became customary to add a commemoration of his sufferings at the end of each Hour; these became known as the Hours of the Cross.[21] This reflects the need for completeness shown by the addition of 'Jesus' to the Hail Mary itself.

The point of emphasizing this liturgical background is to demonstrate that, from its inception, the Hail Mary has nearly always been used to stand in for some more elaborate form of prayer addressed to God himself. In the same way that the Little Office stands in for the canonical Office for devout lay people who could read, and celebrates the whole mystery of salvation, so the Hail Mary itself could stand in for the Little Office for the vast majority of medieval society, who could not read. Thus, the recitation of the 150 psalms of the Psalter, the basic 'prayer book' of the Christian tradition, could be replaced by reciting 150 Hail Marys.[22] These 150 'psalms' could be subdivided into three sets of fifty, to be said at morning, midday and evening.

It is easy to see how the modern practice of the rosary has evolved from this: a complete rosary involves fifteen 'decades', that is, fifteen sets of ten Hail Marys, giving 150 in all; these fifteen decades are subdivided into three sets of five decades, to be said morning, noon and night, which is why a set of rosary beads consists of five sets of ten beads, plus a few extra ones to represent additional prayers such as the Our Father. In addition, the recitation of each decade of the rosary is meant to be accompanied by meditation on a scene from the life of Christ: the five 'joyful mysteries' (the Annunciation, the Visitation to Elizabeth, the birth of Jesus, the Purification, and the finding of the child Jesus in the temple); the five 'sorrowful mysteries' (Christ's agony in Gethsemane, scourging, crowning with thorns, carrying of the cross, and crucifixion); and the five 'glorious mysteries' (the Resurrection, the Ascension, the descent of the Holy Spirit, the Assumption of Mary and her coronation in heaven). Consequently, with the exception of the last two mysteries, the rosary represents a methodical meditation on the whole life of Jesus, thus preserving the ultimately Christ-centred focus of the entire exercise.

The last two mysteries take us into areas of doctrine concerning Mary with which this chapter is not concerned, but this could be a good point at which to ask: why meditate on the life of Christ through the lens of Mary's life? This brings us back to the issue of devotion to Mary providing an accessible point of entry into the whole mystery of Christ. What is it that causes this accessibility?

First, as a human being, with human feelings, Mary is easy for other human beings to identify with. Her most important experiences are those of giving birth to her child and, tragically, watching him die – harrowing experiences that call forth human empathy at a very deep level. Second, this bond of empathy between us and Mary, and between Mary and Christ, helps to establish her as the most obvious intercessor between men and God. Furthermore, it establishes compassion as the hallmark of her response to human prayers for aid. In this, Mary serves to remind people of the compassion in the heart of God, which is, of course, the central message in the life and crucifixion of Christ. Nevertheless, there is something about the language of divinity surrounding Christ that seems to obscure this message from time to time; perhaps, too, the language of masculinity surrounding the Godhead may be a barrier to the total confidence in receiving help and mercy that the female figure of Mary seems to elicit. Finally, the last two 'mysteries' of the rosary illustrate an important function of Mary. They serve to spell out the implications of the ascension: the risen Christ has taken human flesh, human nature, right into the heart of the Godhead, but again, perhaps, it is easier for humans to understand this through the concept of Mary's flesh, which she shares with her Son, being assumed into heaven and crowned there. This underlines the whole emphasis on the humanity and fleshliness of Christ that medieval devotion to Mary served to reinforce.

Before the modern rosary could develop, however, the Hail Mary needed to reach its modern form by the addition of the second part of the prayer: 'Pray for us sinners now and at the hour of our death.' This petition was not officially added until the sixteenth century. It appears in the Sarum Breviary in 1531,[23] and in the Roman Breviary of Pope Pius V in 1568, among others,[24] although the practice had probably developed before then, as suggested by the rather tentative addition of this phrase in a sermon by Bernardino of Siena, preached around 1440.[25]

There is no direct evidence as to why this petition, rather than any other, should have been added on to the Hail Mary, but we can make some educated guesses. If the addition of 'Jesus' to the prayer implied the commemoration of his passion and death, then a reminder of the meditator's own future death is suggested. In addition, it is interesting that this petition creeps in during the period between 1348 and 1665, when Europe was subjected to repeated epidemics of the plague, making the hour of anyone's death extremely uncertain. Then again, the petition finds its way into the official Breviaries in the sixteenth century, the time of the Reformation, and therefore of religious wars and persecutions.

It is in this period, of the Reformation and Counter-Reformation, that the Hail Mary is given its definitive modern form. Similarly, many other devotions were formalized at this time. We have already looked at the rosary,[26] and now we can turn to the Angelus. This was finalized and imposed as a general observance only in the seventeenth century, although three Hail Marys said at the end of the day, accompanied by the ringing of a bell, can be traced back to thirteenth-century Germany.[27]

Recited morning, noon and night – at approximately 6 a.m., midday and 6 p.m. – it again commemorates the very beginning-point of salvation, the Annunciation. The Angelus consists of a sequence of three scriptural texts, each followed by a Hail Mary: 'The Angel of the Lord announced unto Mary, and she conceived by the Holy Ghost;' 'Behold the handmaid of the Lord; be it unto me according to thy word;' 'And the Word was made flesh, and dwelt among us.' It is then rounded off by an ancient prayer,[28] of which the immediate source is probably the Compline Collect of the Little Office of Our Lady, uniting the incarnation and the passion:

We beseech thee, O Lord, pour thy grace into our hearts; that as we have known the incarnation of thy Son Jesus Christ by the message of an angel, so by his cross and passion we may be brought unto the glory of his resurrection.

Once again, therefore, we see the Hail Mary embedded in a devotion that directs the praying Christian to the whole life and function of Christ. Short and attractive, it provided an easy point of entry into these difficult mysteries for the great rank and file of medieval Christians, and still flourishes today. No wonder it was considered one of the three prayers that all Christians should know.

Notes

1 Hilda Graef, *Mary: A History of Doctrine and Devotion*, 2 vols. (London, Sheed & Ward, 1963, 1965), I, p. 230.
2 The prayer was enjoined in a series of provincial and diocesan synods all across Europe, during the course of the late twelfth to fourteenth centuries, the earliest being Paris and Orléans around 1195. See Graef, *Mary*, I, p. 231; *Marienlexikon*, ed. R. Bäumer and L. Scheffczyk (Institutum Marianum, Regensburg, St Ottilien, Eos Verlag, 1988), I, pp. 311–12.
3 For the Latin text of these hymns, see F. J. E. Raby, *The Oxford Book of Medieval Latin Verse* (Oxford, Oxford University Press, 1959), no. 54, 55, pp. 74–76. English translation: *The English Hymnal*, ed. English Hymnal Co. Ltd. (Norwich, Canterbury Press, 1986), no. 78, 79, pp. 134–37.
4 See *Dictionnaire de Spiritualité*, 1, ed. M. Viller, F. Cavallera, J. de Guibert et al. (Paris, Beauchesne, 1937), col. 1162.
5 *Dictionnaire de Spiritualité*, I, p. 1162; English version in Graef, *Mary*, I, p. 230.
6 *Marienlexikon*, I, p. 313; for the texts, see F. E. Brightman (ed.), *Liturgies Eastern and Western*, 2 vols. (Oxford, 1896), I, p. 56, lines 25–27 (Greek text); p. 128, lines 30–32 (Greek text).
7 For a table of the contents of early MSS, see R.-J. Hesbert (ed.), *Corpus Antiphonalium Officii* (Rome, Herder, 1963), I, p. 17 (8a).
8 Baldwin of Ford, *Tractate 7: On the Angelic Salutation*. Latin text: *PL* 204, cols 467–78.

9   *Dictionnaire de Spiritualité*, I, col. 1163. One of the major collectors of miracle stories of the Virgin in the Middle Ages was Gautier de Coincy (1177–1240). For the version of the Hail Mary he was using, see his *Miracles Nostre Dame*, ed. V. F. Koenig (Geneva, Droz, 1955–70), IV, 575–76: 'Le Salu Notre Dame' (poem commenting on the Hail Mary). For some of the best-known stories collected by Gautier, see Gautier de Coincy, *Le Miracle de Théophile*, ed. D. Maillet (Rennes, 1838); *Of the Tumbler of Our Lady and Other Miracles*, tr. A. Kemp-Welch (London, Chatto & Windus, 1908). For a discussion of miracles of the Virgin, see B. Ward, *Miracles and the Medieval Mind* (London, Scolar, 1982), pp. 132–65.

10 *Dictionnaire de Spiritualité*, I, col. 1164.

11 Gregory the Great, *Homilies on the Gospel* 21. Latin Text: *PL* 76, cols 1075–1312. English translation: Santha Bhattacharji, *Reading the Gospels with Gregory the Great* (Petersham, MA, St Bede's Publications, 2001); Gregory the Great, *Forty Gospel Homilies*, tr. David Hurst (Cistercian Studies 123; 2000).

12 Anselm of Canterbury, *Prayers and Meditations*, tr. Benedicta Ward (Penguin Classics; Harmondsworth, Penguin, 1973), Meditation I, p. 224.

13 Baldwin, *On the Angelic Salutation, PL* 204, col. 478.

14 See note 2 above.

15 *Dictionnaire d'Archéologie Chrétienne et de Liturgie*, 12, ed. F. Cabrol and H. Leclercq (Paris, Letouzey et Ané, 1935), cols 2012–14 . For the English manuscripts, see E. S. Dewick (ed.), *Facsimiles of Horae de Beata Maria Virgine from English MSS. of the Eleventh Century* (Henry Bradshaw Society 21; London, 1902).

16 For this festal material of Our Lady, see for example *The Sarum Breviary (1531)*, ed. F. Procter and C. Wordsworth, 3 vols (Cambridge, 1886), 3, cols 234–47 (Annunciation) and 769–808 (Nativity BVM).

17 Respond 1 for Matins of the Purification, *Sarum Breviary*, 3, col. 134.

18 Graef, *Mary*, I, p. 231.

19 Matins, Lesson 2, *Sarum Breviary*, 2, col. 292. For the texts of the Office of Our Lady, see *Sarum Breviary*, 2, cols. 283–314.

20 *The Prymer or Lay Folks' Prayer Book*, ed. H. Littlehales, 2 vols. (Early English Text Society 105, 109; London, 1895, 1897), I, p. 5.

21 For example, see the commemoration of the cross at the end of Lauds, *The Prymer*, I, p. 15.

22 Graef, *Mary*, I, pp. 232–3; *Marienlexikon*, I, p. 311.

23 *Sarum Breviary*, 2, col. 1.

24 *Marienlexikon* I, p. 309.

25 *Dictionnaire de Spiritualité*, I, col. 1164. For the second half of the Hail Mary, see also J. Miller, *Beads and Prayers: The Rosary in History and Devotion* (London, Burns & Oates, 2001), pp. 50–53.

26 For a full history of the rosary, see the article 'Rosencranz' by H. Rzepkowski, in *Marienlexikon* 5, pp. 553–9; also *Dictionnaire de Spiritualité*, 13, cols. 938–80.

27 For the development of the Angelus, see *Marienlexikon*, I, pp. 146–9; *Dictionnaire de Spiritualité*, I, cols. 1164–5).

28 For a history of this prayer's use in England, see Eamonn O Carragáin, 'The Annunciation of the Lord and his Passion: a liturgical topos from St. Peter's on the Vatican in *The Dream of the Rood*, Thomas Cranmer and John Donne,' in *Essays on Anglo-Saxon and Related Themes, in Memory of Lynne Grundy*, ed. J. Roberts and J. Nelson (Kings College Medieval Studies 17; London, 2000), pp. 339–81.

Further reading

Graef, Hilda, *Mary: A History of Doctrine and Devotion*, 2 vols. (London, Sheed & Ward, 1963, 1965).

Juniper, Carol (ed.), *Mariology*, 3 vols. (Milwaukee, WI, Bruce Publishing Co., 1955–61).

Miller, J., *Beads and Prayers: The Rosary in History and Devotion* (London, Burns & Oates, 2001).

Pelikan, Jaroslav, *Mary through the Centuries* (New Haven, CT, Yale University Press, 1996).

5

THE BEATITUDES

JEREMY SHEEHY

Blessed are the poor in heart,
for theirs is the kingdom of heaven.
Blessed are they that mourn,
for they shall be comforted.
Blessed are the meek,
for they shall inherit the earth.
Blessed are they that do hunger and thirst after righteousness,
for they shall be filled.
Blessed are the merciful,
for they shall obtain mercy;
Blessed are the pure in heart,
for they shall see God.
Blessed are the peacemakers,
for they shall be called the children of God.
Blessed are they which are persecuted for righteousness sake,
for theirs is the kingdom of heaven.
Blessed are you when men shall revile you and persecute you
*   and shall say all manner of evil against you for my sake:*
rejoice and be exceeding glad, for great is your reward in
*   heaven, for so persecuted they the prophets which were before you.*

The description of chapters 5 to 7 of St Matthew's Gospel as
'the Sermon on the Mount' seems to go back to Augustine of
Hippo and his exposition of the Sermon. These chapters are
said to be the three most frequently mentioned of the entire
Bible in the early Christian writings, at least as far as those
writings are extant. The isolation within that material of
5.3–10 as 'the Beatitudes' (and the parallel verses in Luke, of
which more below) is found in the Greek Father, Origen, and

in Eusebius of Caesarea, while Gregory of Nyssa's *Homilies* on the Beatitudes treat of and expound them as a unit. The beatitude is a literary form that would have been familiar to the first Christians both from the Hebrew Scriptures and also from Greek literature. In the Old Testament, beatitudes appear especially in the Psalms and the wisdom literature, usually in the third person (e.g. Proverbs 8.34–35, Psalm 1.1–3, Ecclesiasticus 25.7–10). In the Jewish apocalyptic intertestamental literature, there are beatitudes in the second person ('Blessed are you'); and in the New Testament there are other examples of this sort of statement apart from those we usually call 'the Beatitudes'. It is against this background that we hear the Beatitudes of the Gospels.

Makarios, the Greek word used, which is translated 'blessed' or 'happy', suggests a happiness that comes from a right relationship with God. The commentators say that, though it had come to be used without religious overtones in Greek literature, it still carries some flavour of Homer's 'the blessed ones' for the gods. Blessedness belongs to the gods alone, and those who are called blessed in these Beatitudes are not fortunate in any ordinary sense of the word. The satisfactions promised to the blessed are the eschatological gift of God.

The Beatitudes have been used by many writers in the Christian spiritual tradition; they have played a number of roles, and a number of different understandings of them have been adopted. Here, not because of any position about the synoptic witness, but because the focus in the spiritual tradition has been on the Beatitudes as presented in Matthew's Gospel, the focus similarly will be on the Matthean Beatitudes. As Simon Tugwell writes:

> There is no doubt that the beatitudes have played a quite special role in Christian thinking about life. Bossuet places them at the beginning of the meditations which he put together for the use of his Visitation nuns, saying, 'If the sermon on the mount is the précis of all Christian doctrine, the eight beatitudes are the précis of the whole sermon of the mount' (Tugwell, 1980, p. 1).

Yet while Bossuet is clearly trying to emphasize the significance of the Beatitudes, I do not think that his words help us to explain the Beatitudes, to see how others have used them in prayer, or to make them texts for our own prayer. The Sermon on the Mount is not, I would want to argue, helpfully seen as the précis of all Christian doctrine. Nor do the eight Beatitudes appear an accurate précis of the Sermon on the Mount. As Dale Allison puts it in his contribution to the *Oxford Bible Commentary*:

> The Sermon on the Mount is not an adequate or complete summation of anyone's religion . . . It was never intended to stand by itself; it is rather part of a larger whole. The Sermon on the Mount's demands are perverted when isolated from the grace and Christology which appear from Matthew in its entirety (Allison, 2001, p. 852).

What I want to do in this chapter is to look at six understandings of the Beatitudes, and at the way in which each understanding can give rise to a particular way of using the Beatitudes in spirituality and, most importantly, in our prayer.

Augustine wrote his exposition of the Sermon on the Mount, including its treatment of the Beatitudes, quite early in his career. He had been baptized at Easter 387 and returned to Africa in the following year. Valerius, the elderly bishop of Hippo, ordained him priest in 391, and it was soon after that, about the year 393 (before he was consecrated as coadjutor-bishop in 395), that Augustine was able to fulfil his wish to comment on the Sermon on the Mount. For Augustine the Sermon on the Mount is 'a perfect standard of the Christian life' (*DSDM*, I. 1). He sees the Beatitudes as steps to Christian perfection.

According to Augustine's enumeration, there are eight Beatitudes. (He is chiefly interested in the Matthean Beatitudes, as we have noted, and argues in his *Harmony of the Gospels*, II. 19, that there were in the ministry of Jesus two sermons, one set by Matthew on the Mount and the other set by Luke on the plain.) But he points out that the eighth Beatitude 'as it were, returns to the starting-point, because it shows and commends what is complete and perfect . . . Seven in number, therefore are the things which bring perfection: for the eighth brings into light and shows what is perfect' (*DSDM*, I. 3). This enables Augustine to spend a little time displaying his love of numerical symbolism. Eight calls to mind circumcision on the eighth day and the resurrection on the eighth day (which, of course, is also a first day), and the eight days of the baptismal octave, and the very number of Pentecost (because seven times seven is forty-nine, and if you add an eighth one, you get fifty).

Seven, of course, is the golden number, but it also enables Augustine to match the seven Beatitudes to the seven gifts of the Holy Spirit; he also relates these to the seven petitions of the Lord's Prayer (and some medieval writers are able to work in the seven orders of ministry as well!). So, for instance, 'fortitude corresponds to those hungering and thirsting: for they labour in earnestly seeking joy from things that are truly good, and in eagerly seeking to turn away their love from earthly and corporeal things' (*DSDM*, I. 4). The exegesis that establishes Augustine's relationship between a gift of the Spirit and a Beatitude does not always seem wisely established, as when he argues that the mourners are those who, having been converted, are still missing and mourning over the worldly things formerly dear to them, until they are consoled and comforted by the Holy Spirit. Thus Augustine can see a relationship here with the gift of the Holy Spirit that is knowledge, for 'knowledge corresponds to those that mourn who already have found out in the Scriptures by what evils they are held chained which they ignorantly have coveted as though they were good and useful' (*DSDM*, I. 4).

Whatever the weaknesses of the detail of the exegesis, there are several features in Augustine's understanding of the Beatitudes that he was to hand on to others until they became commonplace in the Western Christian tradition: for example, the concept of the Sermon on the Mount itself, the focus on the Matthean text, and the role of the eighth Beatitude as summing up and recapitulating. Augustine had already used what one writer describes as the 'scalar plan' (Lancel, 2002, p. 177), and he would use it soon again. Here are steps to that to which God has called us. What would certainly be used by others and would become part of the pursuit of Christian holiness is the vision of the Beatitudes as a call to a righteousness that goes beyond that of the scribes and Pharisees. Indeed, the Western lectionary tradition has been able to find no reading thought more appropriate than this for the feast of All Saints, for it occurs in the old Roman lectionary, in the Book of Common Prayer and in the various lectionaries dependent on the present Roman lectionary, such as the Revised Common Lectionary and the current Church of England provision. We might call Augustine's understanding that of the Beatitudes as the stairway to sanctity.

If Augustine sees the Beatitudes as a stairway to *sanctity*, we might describe our next writer too as understanding them as a stairway; but not one that leads precisely to holiness of life, Christian perfection and sanctity, but rather to growth in prayer, contemplative life and mystical union. Sanctity should, of course, be an outworking of mystical union, but it is not necessarily so, and there have been those whom the church has hailed as great saints who have not displayed a particular attraction to the contemplative and the mystical in their prayer. The difference should not be overdone, but there is, I think, a difference between the way in which Augustine wants us to use the Beatitudes and the way commended by our next writer, Gregory of Nyssa.

Gregory was born around 330 and was made Bishop of Nyssa in Cappadocia in Asia Minor about 371 (by his brother, Basil, who was trying to safeguard his own authority as Bishop of Caesarea). His *Homilies* on the Beatitudes read like genuine homilies, from a master of the preacher's art, with lots of illustrations from contemporary life and from pagan literature (and also from the medical knowledge of the time). The concern of Gregory is that we should grow in our contemplation of the divine image. Contemplating the divine image in ourselves can form within us a conception of the divine perfections, for we are made in the image and likeness of God. Knowing something of this divine perfection, we shall be able to see more of it and know more of it, and will ourselves grow in the beatitude that is the divine life. Anthony Meredith puts it like this:

> The desire for the vision of God has been subtly transformed into the vision of the purified image of God within the soul. The argument runs as follows: seeing God is the same as having within oneself the purified image of God. The upshot of Gregory's treatment is to connect the vision of God in this life, and probably in that to come, with the perception of the effects of God's activities in the universe and of the moral life in the human soul. It is by virtue that we imitate God in this life and therefore come to share in his nature more fully. Virtue, knowledge and sharing are linked closely together (Meredith, 1995, p. 60).

Gregory makes the distinction (which would become famous in the thinking of the Eastern tradition) between the invisible and unshared essence of God and his energies: 'for he is invisible by nature, but becomes visible in his energies, for he may be contemplated in the things that are referred to him' (*OB*, 6).

This may seem a very individualistic search for the ascent to God, and, furthermore, Gregory can seem to allow little place for the person of Christ. But Gregory does make it clear that this happens through the Word sent by the Father to call us back to the Father: 'the Word that proceeds by successive stages leads us by the hand to the higher steps of the ladder of the Beatitudes' (*OB*, 4). Here are the Beatitudes as the ladder of prayer, the ladder of spiritual ascent, a way of prayer.

Another way of using the Beatitudes is as a spur to penitence. After all, as the French novelist François Mauriac (1937, p. 76) comments, 'every benediction implies a malediction', and we find 'woes' as well as beatitudes in the Sermon on the Mount. The Beatitudes have lent themselves to liturgical use in the penitential rite and in services of celebration of repentance and reconciliation. So, for instance, the Church of England's *Lent, Holy Week and Easter* structures one of its services of penitence

around an examination of conscience that uses the Beatitudes
as the theme:

> Our Lord Jesus Christ said, 'Blessed are the meek, for they
> shall inherit the earth.' We have been angry in our hearts
> and in our words. We have returned evil for evil. We have
> done violence ourselves and condoned the violence of
> others.

And *The Rite of Penance* of the Roman Ritual provides a sample
penitential service entitled 'The Beatitudes', where the act of
repentance is based on the Beatitudes of Matthew's Gospel:

> Lord Jesus Christ, you said: 'Blessed are the poor in spirit, for
> theirs is the kingdom of heaven.' Yet we are preoccupied
> with money and worldly goods and even try to increase them
> at the expense of justice. Lamb of God, you take away the sin
> of the world.

But I find a most striking example of this understanding of the
Beatitudes in the medieval poet Dante Alighieri, who, in that
finest of all Christian allegories, *The Divine Comedy*, gives the
Beatitudes an important role in his second part, on purgatory.
Dante's purgatory is tightly organized and, to the new reader,
complicated. As Dorothy L. Sayers comments in the notes to
her translation:

> Since Purgatory is a place of systematic discipline, it is only to
> be expected that it should be more highly and more serenely
> organized than Hell. Even upon Hell, indeed, the medieval
> passion for order imposes a coherent classification and a
> rigid external symmetry. But within the circles thus ordered,
> the anarchy of evil goes, for the most part, its own chaotic
> way . . . In Purgatory, although the circles are fewer and the
> classification much simpler, the symmetry of the whole is
> more elaborate, and the activity of each circle has a much
> richer content (Sayers, 1955, p. 61).

In Dante's arrangement of purgatory, each circle, or cornice (the poet imagines terraces on a huge mountain in the Antipodes), is devoted to the purging of one of the capital (or 'deadly' sins). On each cornice there is a penance, itself appropriate to the sin, together with a proper meditation, consisting of examples of the sin and of the opposing virtue, and a prayer, appropriate for its purpose, taken from the Psalms or the liturgy. Dante also incorporates the Beatitudes into his scheme; on every cornice, when full measure of purgation is accomplished for any individual, one of the Beatitudes is pronounced as a blessing, sending the individual on his way.

Let me give one example in greater detail of how this works, before commenting further on Dante's use of the Beatitudes. The gluttonous, whose sin is a disordered love of a secondary good, are in penance by hunger (*Purgatory*, Cantos 22–24). They hear of two examples. The first, from classical mythology, tells of the centaurs who were invited to a wedding. Getting very drunk, they attempted to violate the bride and other guests, so that Theseus and others fought them and beat them. The other, from the Old Testament, recounts how Gideon rejected from his army those who, when thirsty, abandoned all precautions while quenching their thirst. They are reminded, as examples of temperance, of Mary's concern for those who gave the feast rather than for herself at the wedding at Cana; of Daniel and his companions, who turned away from rich food so as to keep the dietary laws of the Jews; of John the Baptist in the wilderness, where 'locusts and honey were enough to feed the Baptist in the desert; whence his glory is such, and such his greatness as ye read' (Canto 22, 151ff.). From classical literature they are reminded of how, according at least to Valerius Maximus, the women did not take wine and 'asked no better treat than water for their drink' (Canto 22, 145–6). The prayer is that which opens the canonical Offices in the Western liturgical tradition: 'O Lord, open thou my lips, and my mouth shall show forth thy praise.' This reminds them that the mouth was made for other things beside satisfying the desires of the flesh, and of their part and purpose in the glorification of God. Their blessing, for which

Dante takes some little liberty with the usual text, is 'Blessed are those who hunger after righteousness'.

Dante has seven sins, and he distributes the Beatitudes to the sins in such a way that, as already noted, the gluttonous hear of the blessing of those who hunger after righteousness. The covetous hear of the blessing of those who thirst, because they did not. The proud are moved by hearing of the poor in spirit, while the blessing of the merciful is used for the envious; envy is the opposite of mercy, because to be envious is to regard others wrongly, whereas to be merciful is precisely to see them aright. Wrath is purged so that the blessing of the peacemakers is heard, as one might expect; while perhaps more surprisingly, the Beatitude for the fourth cornice, of the slothful, is the blessing of those who mourn. Dante's thinking here seems to be that those who mourn are promised consolation, and consolation is exactly what the slothful need, because part of the essence of sloth is the refusal of joy and consolation; in extreme forms it culminates in morbid introspection and despair. The emphasis, then, in this case, seems less on the fact of the mourning than on the reward promised. Finally, the lustful, on the seventh cornice, hear the blessing of the pure in heart. Here it is particularly appropriate, because the seventh is the last and final cornice of Mount Purgatory before the entry into Paradise. So Dante makes his arrangements by omitting the Beatitude of the meek, presumably because the wrathful are to hear the Beatitude of the peacemakers (and he does not feel it fits elsewhere) and the Beatitude of those who are persecuted (perhaps this is something done to the blessed rather than something they do). Dante finds the 'extra' beatitude, which is therefore required, by splitting 'hungering for righteousness' and 'thirsting for righteousness'. Perhaps for those of us who are conscious of our lack of spiritual growth and our all too ordinary Christian lives, the use of the Beatitudes to remind us of what we have to be penitent for is particularly useful.

Martin Luther, the Reformation leader, reacts against much of the tradition of understanding the Beatitudes that had developed through the patristic and medieval writers. For Luther, in his treatise *On the Sermon on the Mount*, the Beatitudes

are not a stairway to Christian perfection, a guide to the ascent
to contemplation or a spur to penitence, but a set of rules for
the people of God. Luther takes the Beatitudes at their face
value. The argument seems simple. Luther's understanding of
the Beatitudes depends upon it. If you have to do this to be
blessed, then all those who are to be blessed must be able to do
whatever this is. In part, this was no doubt a reaction against the
domination of so much late medieval Christian life (especially,
perhaps, that in the tradition in which Luther himself had been
taught, and not a domination seen, I would argue, in Dante) by
the standards and expectations of the vowed religious. Against
those who seemed to him to think the Beatitudes relevant only
to the vowed religious, and who made too easy distinctions
between the commandments applicable to all and the so-called
'evangelical counsels' (for instance, of poverty, chastity, and
obedience), Luther wants the Beatitudes to be available to all.
He writes:

> According to them [his Catholic opponents], Christ does not
> intend everything in the fifth chapter to be regarded by his
> Christians as a command for them to observe, but he gave
> much of it merely as advice to those who want to become
> perfect, to be kept by anyone who pleases (Luther, 1956,
> pp. 1–2).

Let us look in more detail at how Luther understands particular Beatitudes. To be spiritually poor means not setting 'confidence, comfort, and trust on temporal goods' (Luther, 1956,
p. 13). This is something to which all are called; and Luther
tells us, moreover, to use all physical necessities and temporal
goods as if guests in a strange place. Because not all mourn in
the usual sense, for Luther's exposition a man is said to mourn
'if he does not depend upon having a good time and living it
up, the way the world does' (p. 19), but instead is grieved by 'so
much wickedness, arrogance, contempt, and blasphemy of God
and his Word' (p. 20). We see the same understanding at work
when we are told that the meekness for which God looks in
those he is to bless is 'to live in human society with meekness

and patience and to hold on to what you have with peace and a good conscience' (p. 24). This meekness is to characterize individuals in their relation to others, and is not meant to apply to those in official positions of authority as rulers and governors. Let me take one more example: the one who hungers and thirsts for righteousness 'works and strives with all his might to promote the general welfare and the proper behaviour of everyone and . . . helps to maintain and support this by word and deed, by precept and example' (p. 26).

In reaction to the captivity of the notion of particular vocation by those who join religious communities or are ordained, Luther seem not to want to set the idea free, but to destroy it. It seems that he expounds the Beatitudes in line with the principle that, if Jesus says such-and-such are to be blessed, then all who are to be blessed must be such-and-such. The Beatitudes become the commandments for the community of Jesus, and must be kept by all. No doubt the aim was to throw the full keeping of the law open to all, and the Beatitudes are understood as a set of rules for all Christians. All are called to these, and this is a gain and a strength; but I suggest that at Luther's hands the Beatitudes lose something of their paradoxical, mysterious, radical quality.

It was perhaps in reaction to the understanding of Luther, which, by throwing open to all the keeping of the Beatitudes, could also seem to remove their challenge and tame their appeal, that our next understanding was developed. The famous pastor of the German Confessing Church and the martyr of the church struggle against Hitler, Dietrich Bonhoeffer, wrote his book *The Cost of Discipleship* in reaction to some such understandings. He was director of the Finkenwalde seminary (first founded at Zingst), and the book derives from lectures on the New Testament to the students. The core of the book is on the Sermon on the Mount. Bonhoeffer comments that, in the fight for the defence of costly grace, the cheap grace to be opposed is 'the grace which amounts to the justification of sin without the justification of the repentant sinner' (Bonhoeffer, 1959, p. 36). The book restores the place of discipleship alongside the Reformed watchwords of faith, justification and sanctification. So, for Bonhoeffer, the Beatitudes outline the cost of discipleship.

> He spoke to men who had already responded to the power of his call, and it is that call which has made them poor, afflicted and hungry. He calls them blessed, not because of their privation, or the renunciation they have made, for these are not blessed in themselves. Only the call and the promise, for the sake of which they are ready to suffer poverty and renunciation, can justify the beatitudes (Bonhoeffer, 1959, p. 96).

As Bonhoeffer interprets the Beatitudes, they show the new community called together. 'With each beatitude the gulf is widened between the disciples and the people, their call to come forth from the people becomes increasingly manifest' (p. 98). Bonhoeffer links the Beatitudes directly to the cross of Christ. This is a christological interpretation of the Beatitudes. Eberhard Bethge, the biographer of Bonhoeffer, writes:

> In the interpretation of the weak Word we are close to the profoundest thought ever expressed by Bonhoeffer: discipleship as participation in Christ's suffering for others, as communion with the Crucified. Here a wealth of personal experience is apparent between the lines. Yet Bonhoeffer succeeds in avoiding both the painful, self-pitying mood found in many hymns, and he avoids also the exaltation of mysticism. The deputizing element in discipleship prevents it from becoming introverted and an end in itself. Disciples are the kind of people who take upon themselves what others would like to shake off (Bethge, 1970, p. 374).

As Bonhoeffer himself puts it:

> Having reached the end of the beatitude, we naturally ask if there is any place on this earth for the community which they describe. Clearly, there is one place, and only one, and that is where the poorest, meekest, and most sorely tried of all men

is to be found – on the cross at Golgotha. The fellowship of
the beatitudes is the fellowship of the Crucified. With him it
has lost all, and with him it has found all. From the cross
there comes the call 'blessed, blessed' (Bonhoeffer, 1959,
p. 103).

This is a christological understanding of the Beatitudes, seeing
them as meant for the community of the disciples, who are
called to 'the fellowship of the Crucified'.

It is in the Orthodox world that the Beatitudes have become
a standard part of the liturgical test. Unfortunately, several of
the standard manuals expounding and explaining the liturgy
do not comment on the significance of the occurrence and
position of the Beatitudes, probably because on various
occasions other tests are used. At Typika (a sort of Office for
days on which the divine liturgy is not celebrated) the Beatitudes are recited, and in the divine liturgy the Beatitudes are
sung on Sundays as the third of the hymns just before the lesser
entrance and the Epistle. But most of the great feasts have their
own proper texts for these hymns, and so the Beatitudes will be
displaced; on weekdays antiphons from the Psalms are used
instead. Some texts comment that in many places the weekday
antiphons are used on Sundays by custom. So the most famous
of the commentaries on the divine liturgy, that by Nicholas
Cabasilas, comments on the antiphons from the Psalms, as does
the modern comprehensive study by Casimir Kucharek.

The Russian novelist Nikolai Gogol was born in 1809 and
died beset by frequent despair in 1852, and is best known for
his novel *Dead Souls* and his play *The Inspector*. Gogol does
discuss the place of the Beatitudes in his commentary on the
divine liturgy, written while he enjoyed a period of warm, keen
Orthodox faith and practice. Here is a liturgical understanding
of the Beatitudes that sees them as part of our pilgrimage
towards the vision of God. Before the gates open for the lesser
entrance (the gates that symbolize for the worshippers the
gates of heaven) and the altar is seen, the words of Christ that
promise entry into the gate of heaven and the sight of God are
recited. And the context is set for the recitation of the Beati-

tudes by the use of the words of the repentant thief at Calvary. The text begins: 'In thy Kingdom remember us, O Lord, when thou comest in thy Kingdom. Blessed are the poor in spirit, for theirs is the kingdom of the heavens . . .' Gogol writes:

> From the choir, for everyone to hear, ring out the beatitudes, proclaiming in this world knowledge of truth and in the world to come life everlasting. The congregation, echoing the cry of the wise thief to Christ upon the cross, 'Remember us, O Lord, when thou comest in thy Kingdom,' repeats after the choir these words of the Saviour (Gogol, 1960, p. 17).

Gogol relates the singing of the Beatitudes to the imminent opening of the doors for the lesser entrance:

> The congregation of the faithful feelingly repeats after the choir these words of the Saviour which declare those who may await and hope for eternal life in the world to come, who are the true kings of peace, the co-heirs and participators in the heavenly kingdom. Now the Royal Gates are solemnly opened, as though they were the gates of the kingdom of heaven itself opening wide, and before the eyes of the worshippers the altar, radiant, stands revealed, like the habitation of the glory of God and the seat of heavenly wisdom whence flows out to us knowledge of truth and the proclamation of eternal life (Gogol, 1960, p. 19).

The Beatitudes function as a promise that is fulfilled symbolically in the course of the rest of the divine liturgy.

Conclusion

We have, then, six different approaches to the Beatitudes. Augustine sees them as a scale for Christian perfection, and Gregory of Nyssa as a stairway to mystical prayer; but Luther reacts against the danger that such approaches may make them seem to be purely for the adept. Dante incorporates them in his poetic description of Mount Purgatory, and no doubt there is a place for using them in our prayer of repentance and reconciliation. Bonhoeffer in his turn appears to react against Luther's emphasis that the Beatitudes are for all, lest it lose their paradoxical scandal. In the Orthodox liturgical tradition, finally, we are reminded of their essentially eschatological nature, of the blessing of the vision of God promised to the people of God. These are different approaches, but they have in common the conviction that Christians are called to be people of the Beatitudes.[1]

Note

1 As I was finishing this chapter in July 2002, the World Youth Day was taking place with Pope John Paul II in Toronto, and I noticed that the theme of much of the worship centred on the call to be the people of the Beatitudes.

References

Allison, Dale C., Jr. (2001). *Matthew.* The Oxford Bible Commentary; Oxford, Oxford University Press.

Augustine, *Our Lord's Sermon on the Mount* (*DSDM*).

Bethge, Eberhard (1970). *Dietrich Bonhoeffer.* London, Collins.

Bonhoeffer, Dietrich (1959). *The Cost of Discipleship.* London, SCM Press.

Gogol, N. V. (1960). *The Divine Liturgy of the Russian Orthodox Church.* London, Darton, Longman and Todd.

Gregory of Nyssa, *On the Beatitudes* (*OB*).

Kucharek, C. (1971). *The Byzantine-Slav Liturgy of St John Chrysostom.* Combermere, Canada, Alleluia Press.

Lancel, Serge (2002). *St Augustine.* London, SCM Press.

Lent, Holy Week, Easter (1984). London, Church House Publishing.

Luther, Martin (1956). *On the Sermon on the Mount.* Tr. J. Pelikan, and quoted from *Luther's Works,* XXI. St Louis, MI, Concordia.

Mauriac, François (1937). *Life of Jesus.* London, Hodder & Stoughton.

Meredith, Anthony (1995). *The Cappadocians.* London, Geoffrey Chapman.

The Rite of Penance (1976). London, Collins.

Sayers, Dorothy L. (tr. and ed.) (1955). *Dante: The Divine Comedy 2: Purgatory.* Harmondsworth, Penguin.

Tugwell, S. (1980). *The Beatitudes: Soundings in Christian Traditions.* Springfield, MO, Templegate.

6

PSALM 23

GORDON MURSELL

The LORD is my shepherd, I shall lack nothing.
He makes me lie down in green pastures,
and leads me beside still waters.
He restores my soul.
He leads me in the paths of righteousness
for his name's sake.
Yes, though I walk through the valley of the shadow of death,
I will fear no evil, for you are with me;
your rod and staff comfort me.
You prepare a table before me
in the presence of my enemies;
you anoint my head with oil; my cup runs over.
Surely goodness and mercy will follow me
all the days of my life,
and I shall dwell in the house of the LORD for ever.

The twenty-third psalm is one of the best-known and most influential prayers ever written; and since, like all the psalms, it will have formed part of the foundation of Jesus' own spiritual life, its motifs and imagery (supremely the image of God as shepherd) may plausibly be considered as influential in the development of his own self-understanding. And yet even a cursory glance at its deceptively simple text and structure will show that, like many other psalms, it has a character that is entirely different from almost every other genre of Christian prayer. The psalmist begins by talking *about* God ('The LORD is my shepherd'), and then moves seamlessly into dialogue *with* God ('you are with me, your rod and your staff comfort me'). By the end of the last verse, we have returned to talk *about* God again ('I shall dwell in the house of the LORD for ever'). Prayer (talking with God) is framed by theology (talking about God). The psalmist can see no reason to separate the two.

Unfortunately for the spiritual health of Western Christianity, most other writers *have* separated them. There is much argument about whether the split between theology and prayer is the result of the ever-increasing schematizing of the late scholastic theologians, or a near-inevitable consequence of the Enlightenment, driving theology away from the pew and into the arms of secular academic disciplines. Both were far from the spiritual world of the psalmist. For him or her, it was the most natural thing in the world to hold together what you believe with how you pray. On one level, this is obvious enough: the kind of God we believe in is the one to whom we pray. But this holding together has decisive consequences: for if, as in the Psalms, it is of the very essence of good prayer to draw the whole of life into our relationship with God – including the heights of our joy and the depths of our despair – then that prayer will influence our theology, and vice versa. Neither can any longer be smooth or untroubled affairs, easily controlled by religious authorities or left entirely to the arguments of academics. In the earthy directness of the twenty-third psalm, the barriers between pew and academy, between synod and street, are subverted – to the inestimable advantage of them all.

This underlines an important feature of the spirituality of the Psalms. Whether or not we accept the ancient ascription of many psalms (including the twenty-third) to King David, the principle behind that association matters. David was many things: a shepherd, a fighter, a ruler, a rebel, a family man and a murderous adulterer. But he certainly was not a clergyman. The twenty-third psalm breathes the air, not of the church, but of the countryside. Not all of its many imitators have sufficiently esteemed that fact. Thus it was, perhaps, natural for St Augustine to connect the 'still waters' of verse 2 with the liturgy of baptism.[1] But there is loss as well as gain once we accept Coverdale's subtly moralized translation of the same phrase as 'waters of comfort', which appears also in the (otherwise largely accurate) Scottish metrical version, 'The Lord's my Shepherd'.

George Herbert is closer to the original with his 'streams that gently pass', as is Gordon Jackson with his 'clearest brooks',[2] but even Herbert will later intrude a hint of Calvinism with his 'and all this not for my desert, But for his holy name'. And Henry Williams Baker will either christianize or ecclesiasticize (depending on one's point of view) the entire psalm in his 'The King of Love my Shepherd is', in which the picnic table becomes 'food celestial', the cup of wine 'thy pure chalice', and the local shepherd none other than Christ himself.

It is too easy to criticize these approaches: the original Hebrew is itself by no means free from ambivalence and uncertainty. In verse 3, for example, the Lord could as easily be understood as guiding me in 'right [in the sense of going in the right direction] paths' as in 'paths of righteousness'. And the entire psalm, which appears to be the prayer of an Israelite agricultural worker, can, as we have seen, be no less legitimately read as the prayer of the king. Good prayer, like great art, is not restricted to any one interpretation: *cor ad cor loquitur*. We must beware only of those renderings that fatally narrow, or even homogenize, the broad perspectives of the original.

And one of the ways in which so much modern liturgical and spiritual material does just this is by encouraging the person praying to leave most of his or her life behind when turning to prayer. The most obvious sign of this is a purely grammatical one: the Psalms are full of question marks ('why have you forsaken me?'), while the collects of Gelasius, Cranmer and their liturgical successors speak only in the language of statements and certainty. On the face of it, Psalm 23 does so too. But here also, appearances may be deceptive. Rabbi Jonathan Magonet has pointed to the ambivalence beneath the surface of the little word 'surely' that begins the psalm's closing verse. It appears to breathe the air of sunny confidence. But the same Hebrew word, *ach*, opens the terrible seventy-third Psalm, where it is soon apparent that there is nothing 'sure' about religious faith at all: it is always a demanding engagement with doubt.[3] In Psalm 23, the person praying may be expressing not so much an effortless conviction about the presence of God's covenanted goodness and loving mercy as a gnawing anxiety that these vital gifts may vanish just when they are most urgently needed.

In his powerful and moving composition *Exil*, written in 1994, the Georgian composer Giya Kancheli has set Psalm 23 as the centrepiece of a searching evocation of the spirituality of exile. For him, the 'valley of the shadow of death' is precisely the journey of the exile or refugee; and 'those that trouble me' are the haunting memories that have both nourished and afflicted him ever since he left his own native land. In that context, the last line of the psalm ('I will dwell in the house of the LORD for ever') is no calm confidence, but the passionate, even desperate, prayer of the exile to be able to go home. As always in the Bible, there can be no question of going *back* home: as the prophet Jeremiah makes clear, those exiles who would eventually return to Jerusalem from Babylon would find that God was doing a new thing there (cf. Jeremiah 31.31–34). The heavenly city of Revelation is quite different from the Garden of Eden, just as the 'house of the LORD' that ends the twenty-third psalm is not at all the same as the 'green pastures' that begins it. For the person praying this psalm, 'home' is always on ahead; and nostalgia is not an option.

It is in just such a context that Psalm 23 reveals its fullest potential. For the image of God as shepherd makes God too into a nomad, perennially tramping the hillsides in search of sheep who are trapped or lost. This God is no prisoner of synagogue or church, but someone infinitely more important: a guide on the journey of exile, a companion and a protector. What that God provides is not insurance against exile, but food and drink for the journey, and an enduring hope in its final destination. Seen in this light, Augustine's interpretation of verse 2 as baptismal and of verse 5 as eucharistic need imply no narrowing of perspectives: the whole life of the Christian is a costly and often hazardous journey, through places where we do not wish to be and where we are not in control; and only a God who keeps us company on such a journey (and who, for Christians, has travelled it himself) is credible.

Even so, the journey is not all in exile: there are oases of hospitality *en route*. The God of the twenty-third psalm is not interested only in furious activism: 'he makes me lie down in green pastures, and leads me beside still waters'. This is the God of the sabbath, and even in exile we must keep sabbath time with him; for the sabbath is not just *rest* but *restoration*, and in Scripture that restoration is no heritage-style obsession with the past but the opening-up of an otherwise undreamed-of, and hence subversive, future – subversive because it challenges the seeming inevitability of the present, and both an easy apathy in accepting it and a dangerous activism that presupposes that you alone can change it. 'The Sabbath', wrote the thirteenth-century Rabbi Moses de Leon, 'is a mirror of the world to come';[4] and the twenty-third psalm hints at its transforming power. George Herbert captures this perfectly:

> He leads me to the tender grass,
>   Where I both feed and rest;
> Then to the streams that gently pass:
>   In both I have the best.

Herbert also captures vividly the subversive power of the fifth verse, though his rendering is oddly absent from most hymnbooks:

> Nay, thou dost make me sit and dine,
>   Ev'n in my enemy's sight:
> My head with oil, my cup with wine
>   Runs over day and night.

This is a picnic, but a defiant one: nothing is more calculated to infuriate one's enemies than to take one's ease in full view of them. And the point is the same whether the 'enemies' represent a real and physical threat, or all those interior demons that keep encouraging us to abandon either our journey or the God who travels it with us. This is the crazy but infectious boldness that led the apostles Peter and John to dismiss the demands of the religious authorities (Acts 4.19–20), and that moved generations of later Jews and Christians to celebrate the victory of their God even when – in fact, precisely when – it appeared as though it was the devil who had won. The twenty-third psalm is one of the shortest in the book; but the journey it encompasses is one of the longest. Like Bunyan's pilgrim, fearing neither goblin nor foul fiend, the person who travels with this prayer in his or her spiritual rucksack has no illusions either about the long haul that lies ahead, or the nature and character of the nomadic God who travels too. There is no easy piety here: only essential sustenance for a strenuous but enthralling adventure.

Notes

1   See his *Expositions of the Psalms* (*Enarrationes in Psalmos*) on Psalm 22 (23), and his *Sermon* 366.3.

2   Herbert, 'The 23d [*sic*] Psalm' ('The God of Love my Shepherd is'), from *The Temple*; Gordon Jackson, *The Lincoln Psalter* (Manchester, Carcanet, 1997).

3   Jonathan Magonet, *A Rabbi Reads the Psalms* (London, SCM Press, 1994), p. 67.

4   Moses de Leon, *Zohar*, Genesis 48a; quoted in T. C. Eskenazi, D. J. Harrington and W. H. Shea (eds), *The Sabbath in Jewish and Christian Traditions* (New York, Crossroad, 1991), p. x.

7

HYMNS OF CHARLES WESLEY

RALPH WALLER

Charles Wesley, the younger brother of John, was born in the Epworth Rectory in Lincolnshire in 1707. The household in which Charles grew up was controlled by a strict but stimulating regime. Although an older brother, Samuel, was away at school, Charles had not only John as his companion but also his sisters, whose company and conversation he greatly enjoyed. He went to Winchester School and then to Christ Church College, Oxford. His pattern of work at Oxford was not unlike that of many students in every generation, in that he seems to have made a good start, then socialized too much; but in his last year he worked extremely hard, doing sufficiently well to graduate and to be offered a lectureship at Christ Church.

While John was away from Oxford in 1729, acting as his father's curate, Charles assembled a small group of students who pledged themselves to read together, study the Bible and regularly attend services of Holy Communion. This was the beginning of the 'Holy Club' and when John returned to Oxford he took over the leadership of this small society.

The death of Charles's father, Samuel, in 1735 broke up the family home at Epworth, and within a few months Charles had set out with John for the new colony of Georgia in America. The stormy three-month journey to America had a profound effect on both John and Charles, especially the hymn-singing of the Moravian Christians, which proved to be an effective vehicle for sharing and reinforcing the faith and instilling a sense of corporate bravery in the face of adversity. In Georgia, Charles, who had been recently ordained before leaving England, acted as secretary to Colonel Oglethorpe, the Governor, who was based at Frederica, while John was stationed at Savannah a hundred miles away.

Charles did not have the determination or the stamina of John, and so, having put up with hardship, aggression from disgruntled settlers and ill health, he resigned and returned to England. He left behind his contribution toward a hymnbook published by John in 1737, and entitled *A Collection of Psalms and Hymns*. This was the first hymnbook to be published in North America and set the scene for the many hymnbooks that followed. On his return home, Charles sought out the Moravians in London and, largely through their encouragement, started to rebuild his life. On Whit Sunday 1738 he passed through an experience similar to that of John, but three days earlier. He was ill in bed, but was quickly cured and immediately wrote the hymn 'Where shall my wandering soul begin'. This evangelical conversion empowered his creative spirit, and from that time onwards poetry and hymns continually flowed from his pen. Frank Baker estimates that he wrote some 6,500 hymns, with an additional 3,000 fragments of hymns and verses in manuscript. Many of his hymns were written on cards while riding his horse; there are several stories of him rushing into a house and asking for pen and paper to write down a hymn that had been developing in his mind as he travelled.

Uniquely in the history of the Christian Church, the two brothers John and Charles became the leaders of a great religious movement. They worked closely together, they preached the same message, and when one was in danger the other would come to his help. They faced hostility and persecution with the same steadfastness and courage. Although Charles had a quieter and more settled life than John, in the great theological storms that engulfed them soon after their conversions Charles stood side by side with his brother. Together they faced the challenge of the Moravian doctrine of 'stillness', and together they championed Arminianism against George Whitefield's Calvinism. Charles played a key role in the Evangelical Revival, not only through his hymns but also in his preaching, witness and pastoral care. There were disagreements between the two brothers on such issues as Charles's opposition to John's ordaining ministers for America, and Charles's insistence that Methodism should remain in the

Church of England. But even through these differences the two brothers remained on good terms and in a close relationship.

On one occasion, while travelling in Wales, Charles stayed with the Gwynne family at Garth. His sermons were greatly appreciated by members of the family and he soon became attracted to Sarah, one of the daughters of the household. There were several obstacles in the way of the two marrying, including an age gap of over twenty years and Charles's lack of an income. John came to the rescue, however, by promising an annual stipend to Charles, and the two were married in 1749. Of all Samuel and Susanna Wesley's children, Charles was the only one who enjoyed a long and happy marriage. After a few years as a travelling preacher he limited his ministry to the Bristol area, where he and Sarah had made their home. In 1771 he moved to London, where he lived in Marylebone. Here he arranged musical evenings at which his sons would entertain visitors. In the last years of his life he preached mainly in the London area and exercised a pastoral ministry at West Street Chapel. Until the end of his life he visited the sick and those in prison, and his final hymns were written for condemned prisoners. He died in 1788 and was buried in the Marylebone Parish Churchyard, where his grave can still be seen today.

Charles Wesley's hymns have been over-generously compared to other works of religious art such as King's College Chapel, Cambridge, and Leonardo da Vinci's painting of the Last Supper.[1] The Wesley brothers' hymnbook of 1780 is, however, universally recognized as one of the great contributions to hymnody, due in no small part to the fact that the vast majority of its hymns were written by Charles. James Martineau, the nineteenth-century philosopher and theologian, saw the Wesley hymns as the greatest treasure in Christendom next to the Bible. Other writers too have drawn attention to Bernard Manning's assessment of the 1780 hymn book: 'This little book . . . ranks in Christian literature with the Psalms, the Book of Common Prayer and the Canon of the Mass.'[2]

Charles wrote hymns for almost every occasion, and there is hardly an event in the Christian life for which he did not produce a hymn. There were hymns for baptism and holy

communion, for marriage and conversion. He wrote hymns for
Christmas and Easter, Pentecost and Ascension. His hymns also
reflected the social and political life of his day, including the
Gordon riots and the English earthquake of 1750. He wrote
hymns for the king and a hymn of thanksgiving when Bonnie
Prince Charlie was defeated at the Battle of Culloden. His great
outpouring of hymns included those written for children and
for the miners of Kingswood and Newcastle.

Among so many hymns it was not surprising that some were
discarded because they contained questionable theology or
were poorly constructed. But many of the hymns contained a
deep devotional element that has crossed the centuries and still
speaks to the very heart of the individual believer, conveying
goodness, truth and beauty. The singing of these hymns
touched people at a deeper level than words alone could ever
do, and the congregations who sang them felt humbler and
braver, stronger in their faith and closer to God. Charles's
hymns were sung not only at great gatherings of people, but
also in the home at family worship, and by individuals, like John
Wesley himself, who found that singing hymns on his own
deepened his spiritual life.

Why did Charles's hymns have such an effect? In the first
place, they were steeped in biblical imagery. Almost every line
of his hymns was taken from a biblical image or can be traced
back to a scriptural reference. Indeed, his hymns are so
saturated by Scripture that Ernest Rattenbury once suggested
that, if the Bible were lost, then great sections of it could be
reconstructed from Charles Wesley's hymns.[3] Such a statement,
however, completely overlooks the fact that Charles's hymns
drew on images and words from the Bible that were sometimes
taken at random and out of context; these texts and images he
wove into a tapestry that depicted a deep Christian message.
The same consolidation of biblical imagery that enabled the
Book of Common Prayer to stand the test of time is found also
in Charles's hymns and is part of their classical appeal.

Second, in the Wesley hymns many people have found an
echo of their own deepest needs; the need for forgiveness and
love as well as security in a rapidly changing and uncertain

world. 'Captain of Israel's host, and Guide' would be an example of a hymn equally relevant if it had been sung in the Napoleonic wars, the First World War or after the tragedy of the World Trade Centre.

> Beneath thy shadow we abide
> The cloud of thy protecting love;
> Our strength, thy grace, our rule, thy word;
> Our end, the glory of the Lord.[4]

At his very best, Charles was able to capture in hymns the innermost needs and the deep religious experience of the people of his day, which found an echo in the lives of later generations.

Third, Charles wrote hymns that declared the Nicene faith. While the Churches of England and Rome safeguarded their orthodoxy through the recital of the creeds, Charles wrote hymns that enabled Methodists to sing the orthodox faith. Many of the hymns he wrote on christology and the incarnation are well known and would be sung at services of holy communion and at carol services. His collection of *Hymns on the Trinity* were also an important contribution to the singing of the Nicene faith.

Fourth, in his hymns Charles uses the two most common images of the Christian life, that of fighting and that of pilgrimage. There are numerous hymns on the theme of combat. The hymn 'And are we yet alive' serves as an example of this theme:

> What troubles have we seen
> What conflicts have we passed
> Fightings without, and fears within,
> Since we assembled last!

> But out of all the Lord
> Hath brought us by his love.[5]

This hymn was written for Wesley's conference of preachers, which met amid mob violence and persecution. It is still sung at the opening of the Methodist Conference, but today it is associated more with the inner fighting of the Christian life than with actual persecution.

The idea of the Christian life as a journey is also deeply embedded in Charles's hymns. They contain such lines as: 'Come let us anew Our journey pursue.'[6] The notion that we are not just marking time but are journeying on to heaven and to God is a strong theme. The hymns themselves are often constructed in such a way as to portray a journey. In singing a Charles Wesley hymn, a congregation can be taken on a pilgrimage that does not simply go round in circles, but which starts on earth and ends in heaven. Examples are 'What shall I render to my God?',[7] or those that begin in disbelief and conclude with certainty, such as 'And can it be that I should gain an interest in the Saviour's blood?'[8]

Lastly, Charles's hymns are an anthology of practical divinity. He seldom wrote hymns devoted to abstract theology, but almost always drew out of the great theological theme a practical application for the life of the individual, or an invitation to respond to the Word of God, or a call to serve the present age. Wesley's call to action or belief is reinforced by some of the hymns being written in the first person; this method relates theology more personally to the individual singer, even when they are singing in a large congregation.

The two hymns I have chosen to look at more closely represent two aspects of Charles Wesley's writings. 'Christ the Lord is risen today' is his greatest Easter hymn and is concerned with the central facts of the Christian faith, of God working in history and empowering the resurrection. The second hymn, 'Love divine', is to do with the activity of God in the human heart and our response to God's love. The two approaches are not, of course, mutually exclusive. In Wesley's writing the great events of Easter call for a human response, and the activity of God in the human heart is bound up with the doctrine of incarnation.

Christ the Lord is risen today: *alleluia!*
Sons of men and angels say: *alleluia!*
Raise your joys and triumphs high: *alleluia!*
Sing, ye heavens; thou earth, reply: *alleluia!*

Love's redeeming work is done,
Fought the fight, the battle won;
Vain the stone, the watch, the seal;
Christ hath burst the gates of hell:

Lives again our glorious King;
Where, O death, is now thy sting?
Once he died our souls to save;
Where's thy victory, boasting grave?

Soar we now where Christ hath led,
Following our exalted Head;
Made like him, like him we rise;
Ours the cross, the grave, the skies:

King of Glory! Soul of bliss!
Everlasting life is this,
Thee to know, thy power to prove,
Thus to sing, and thus to love.[9]

The first verse commences with the great statement at the heart
of the Christian faith: 'Christ the Lord is risen today.' The verse
calls for joint rejoicing in heaven and on earth. There is an
image here like the muffled peal of bells ringing on earth and
being answered in heaven. The Easter joy is a shared joy of both
heaven and earth; between humanity on earth and angels in
heaven. Neither heaven nor earth is sufficient alone to express
the magnitude of this event. Both are needed. The joyful news
is sung in heaven, and earth replies.[10] This is such good news
that it needs to be broadcast much more loudly; it is not to be
whispered in gardens, but sung from the rooftops.

The second verse reminds us that everything done by God
has been done in the name of love and for love. 'Fought the

fight, the battle won' refers to St Paul, who speaks of himself as having fought the fight (2 Timothy 4.7). But there is also an allusion here to Christ as the second Adam, the representative of all humankind, who came to the fight, and who, on the cross, took on the worst that sin and evil could do, and triumphed over them. The rest of verse two asserts that nothing could prevent Christ's resurrection and thwart the power of God; not the stone over the tomb, nor the soldiers keeping watch, nor the sealing of the tomb, or even the gates of hell.[11]

Verse three comes to the heart of Easter and the resurrection; that Jesus, our glorious King, is alive and reigns for ever. Even the pain and suffering and misery caused by death are removed, not only in the life of Christ, but through the resurrection of Christ for all people. Line three of the third verse asserts one of the central themes of the Christian faith: that Christ died to save our souls. The lack of any further elaboration or explanation of this event does imply that, in this life, we can never fully understand how this happened, but we simply cling to the fact that it did happen. The verse concludes with the assertion that the victory no longer belongs to death, as it appeared to do on that first Good Friday; with Easter morning and the resurrection, the victory belongs to life.

Verse four is concerned with following in Christ's footsteps. When Roger Bannister ran a mile in under four minutes he showed that it was possible to do it and opened the way for others to repeat his achievement. In a much greater and deeper sense, Christ's resurrection has opened the way for all people to follow him.[12] It is Christ who leads the way to a higher life symbolized by the resurrection. The hymn asserts that, because we are made in his image, we also, like him, shall rise from the dead,[13] but like Christ we shall first have to face both the cross and the grave before we can rise to heaven.[14]

The last verse reasserts that the risen, ascended Christ is the King of glory[15] and that he has achieved everlasting life for all people. This is brought about in the lives of individuals as they come to know Christ and allow his power to be shown through them.[16] The concluding line of this hymn reminds us that the great miracle of the resurrection should be not only told, but sung, so that words and music can combine to capture an event so incredible that words alone are insufficient to convey its magnitude. Finally, the event of the resurrection not only needs to be told and sung, but will also inspire love in our lives as a response to the love we have received from God.

This hymn was first printed in *Hymns and Sacred Poems* of 1739. It is a commentary on 1 Corinthians 15 and based on the accounts of the resurrection in Matthew 28; Mark 16; Luke 24 and John 20.

We turn now to our second Wesley hymn:

> Love divine, all loves excelling,
> Joy of heaven to earth come down,
> Fix in us thy humble dwelling,
> All thy faithful mercies crown.
> Jesu, thou art all compassion,
> Pure, unbounded love thou art;
> Visit us with thy salvation,
> Enter every trembling heart.
>
> Come, almighty to deliver,
> Let us all thy life receive;
> Suddenly return, and never,
> Never more thy temples leave.
> Thee we would be always blessing,
> Serve thee as thy hosts above,
> Pray, and praise thee, without ceasing,
> Glory in thy perfect love.
>
> Finish then thy new creation,
> Pure and spotless let us be;
> Let us see thy great salvation,
> Perfectly restored in thee:
> Changed from glory into glory,
> Till in heaven we take our place,
> Till we cast our crowns before thee,
> Lost in wonder, love and praise![17]

This great hymn records a journey. It starts with the love of God coming down to earth; this is a clear reference to the incarnation, to a God who comes to us even if we cannot get to him on our own. The hymn ends in heaven with all of us in front of the throne of God, lost in wonder, love and praise. It is not about the journey of Christ through his life and death and resurrection, but rather about God working in our lives and inspiring the human journey from earth to heaven.

When Charles Wesley wrote this hymn it had four verses, but in 1780 John Wesley dropped the original verse two because of its controversial nature in regard to the complicated issue of the second blessing.[18] The resultant three-verse hymn (or, in the case of *Hymns Ancient and Modern*, the six-verse hymn of four lines per verse) is much better balanced and has probably become the best known and most loved of all Charles Wesley's hymns. It falls neatly into three sections: a prayer to Jesus to visit the human heart; the receiving of life in all its fullness, so that the redeemed person can praise and glory in the love of God; and finishing the new creation within the life of the individual, which process becomes complete in the full glory of heaven.

In verse one, the first two lines refer to Isaiah 57.15, and tell of the love of God, which is greater than any other love, taking the initiative and coming down to earth from heaven. The following lines emphasize that this love brings with it a joy that is experienced in heaven. Wesley could also be thinking of the central figure of heaven, God himself, who is the cause of all the joy in heaven. Lines five and six refer to love seen in and coming through Jesus. So it focusses not on the wrath of God visiting his people, but on the love of God present in the caring and compassionate Jesus. In him we get a glimpse of the love of God which is pure and not mixed with any kind of selfish interest. Moreover, the love of God is 'unbounded', not limited in its height and depth, breadth and length and its capacity to endure. The last two lines of the first verse are in the form of a corporate prayer that God, who brings salvation and has come down to earth for each of us, should enter every heart.[19] The theological notion here is that God is active in his world by working through the human heart. God gains access to the human heart, however, only through the decision of each individual who allows him to enter. Wesley added the word 'trembling', which he took from Deuteronomy 28.65, in order to capture something of the enormity of the almighty and infinite love of God entering into the life of an individual.

Verse two makes the obvious point that, if the life of God enters and fills our lives, then those lives will be completely transformed.[20] If the life of God truly dwells within us, we shall be delivered not from the ordinary humdrum things of life, but from sin and selfishness, from greed and envy, from bitterness and hatred. Line four, which refers to Malachi 3.1, suggests that we shall be transported to the temples of the Lord. There is an important theological point here that eternal life is not necessarily everlasting life, in the sense of length of life, but is a quality of life lived with God, which begins here and now and continues after death. The remaining lines of the second verse encapsulate something of the purpose of life, which is to glorify God and enjoy him for ever. Once again, heaven and earth are joined together in this purpose, which involves prayer and praise[21] and enjoyment of God's perfect love.

In the final verse the new creation is not the world or the universe, but the human being whose imperfections and blemishes have been removed. In line three the hymn continues as a prayer, asking that we may see the salvation of God, which Wesley perceived as the perfect restoration of the relationship between Almighty God and the whole of humanity. Human beings will be changed to such an extent that we shall be able to take our place in heaven. In the middle of the sixteenth century, the Emperor Charles V renounced all his titles to spend his last years in a monastery. The painter Titian portrayed the scene of a church crowded with nobles, in which the proud titles of the Emperor were read out one by one. But against the background of God, the Holy Trinity, it seemed to count for very little. There is something of that feeling in the last lines of this hymn: as we take our place in heaven, all our earthly achievements count for nothing in the presence of Almighty God; we are simply and completely lost in wonder, love and praise.

Notes

1 Bernard L. Manning, *The Hymns of Wesley and Watts* (London, Epworth Press, 1942), p. 14.
2 Manning, *Hymns*, p. 14.
3 J. R. Watson, *The English Hymn* (Oxford, Clarendon Press, 1997), p. 230.
4 *Hymns and Psalms: A Methodist and Ecumenical Hymn Book* (London, Methodist Publishing House, 1983), no. 62.
5 *Hymns and Psalms*, no. 707.
6 *Hymns and Psalms*, no. 354.
7 *Hymns and Psalms*, no. 703.
8 *Hymns and Psalms*, no. 216.
9 *Hymns and Psalms*, no. 193.
10 Isaiah 49.13.
11 Matthew 16.18.
12 Colossians 3.1.
13 1 John 3.2.
14 Romans 6.4–6.
15 Psalm 24.7.
16 John 17.3.
17 *Hymns and Psalms*, no. 267.
18 See J. R. Watson, *An Annotated Anthology of Hymns* (Oxford, Oxford University Press, 2002), pp. 195–7, for a detailed and authoritative discussion of the missing verse.
19 Psalm 106.4 and Deuteronomy 28.65.
20 John 10.10.
21 1 Thessalonians 5.17.

8

THE BATTLE HYMN
OF THE REPUBLIC

J. R. WATSON

Mine eyes have seen the glory of the coming of the Lord;
He is trampling out the vintage where the grapes of wrath are stored;
He hath loosed the fateful lightning of his terrible swift sword;
　　His truth is marching on.
Glory, glory, Alleluya! . . .

I have seen him in the watch-fires of a hundred circling camps;
They have builded him an altar in the evening dews and damps;
I have read his righteous sentence by the dim and flaring lamps:
　　His day is marching on.
Glory, glory, Alleluya! . . .

I have read a fiery gospel, writ in burnished rows of steel:
'As ye deal with my contemners, so with you my grace shall deal;
Let the hero born of woman crush the serpent with his heel,
　　Since God is marching on.'
Glory, glory, Alleluya! . . .

He hath sounded forth the trumpet that shall never call retreat;
He is sifting out the hearts of men before his judgement-seat;
O, be swift, my soul, to answer him; be jubilant, my feet!
　　Our God is marching on.
Glory, glory, Alleluya! . . .

In the beauty of the lilies Christ was born across the sea,
With a glory in his bosom that transfigures you and me;
As he died to make men holy, let us die to make men free,
　　While God is marching on.
Glory, glory, Alleluya! . . .

[*He is coming like the glory of the morning on the wave;*
He is wisdom to the mighty, he is succour to the brave;
So the world shall be his footstool, and the soul of time his slave;
   Our God is marching on.
Glory, glory, Alleluya! . . .]

The lines that begin 'Mine eyes have seen the glory of the coming of the Lord' have become famous throughout the world, even though they were written on a specific occasion, in a republic proud of its republicanism, to encourage soldiers in a particular campaign. The words inscribe a particular occasion using a particular code, but they have been taken over and re-encoded in ways that have allowed them to cross national boundaries. The phrases have become reverberative, almost legendary: they lie around in American literature like seeds, from which spring up new growths of fiction and history. As a poem it has transcended its originating impulses, although it cannot be understood fully without them; it has detached itself from its republicanism to be found in countries where there are still kings and queens; and it has travelled from its first writing, in the early dawn of a November morning in Willard's Hotel in Washington, to the far corners of the earth.

The author, Julia Ward Howe, was born in New York in 1819, into a distinguished family that came from Rhode Island, where her great-grandfather, Samuel Ward, had been the governor. He was one of those who refused to enforce the Stamp Act, which led to the Revolution of 1776. Her grandfather was a soldier in the War of Independence that followed, and she was always proud to recall that a handwriting expert said of her: 'You inherit military blood; your hand shows it.'[1] Her father was not a soldier; he was a banker in New York, well-to-do and mindful of his civic responsibilities (he was one of the founders of New York University). Her mother died in childbirth when Julia was five years old, so that her childhood was deeply influenced by her father and brothers, and by such nurses and governesses as were brought in to look after her and educate her. She recalled that it was a home in which the old New England Puritanism was a daily reality, or (as she put it) a place 'most

122

carefully and jealously guarded from all that might be represented in the orthodox trinity of evil, the world, the flesh, and
the devil'.[2] Wine was forbidden, and smoking discouraged. For-
tunately, she found allies in her attempts to discover herself in
such an atmosphere: these were her brothers, and friends such
as Charles King, editor of a daily paper called *The New York
American* and later president of Columbia College. King, who
had been at Harrow with Byron, admired Julia's father,
although he was (in her words) 'as convivial in his tastes as my
father was the reverse'. He once called at the house to find a
Temperance Committee meeting going on in the large drawing
room, and amused Julia by saying: 'How I should like to open
those folding doors just wide enough to fire off a bottle of
champagne at those temperance folks!'[3]

As a well-connected New Yorker, she came to meet some of
the great men and women of the time: Washington Irving,
Edgar Allan Poe, Anna Jameson, the Longfellows (Samuel and
Henry Wadsworth), Charles Dickens on his visit. She read
widely, although she remembered that 'the reading of Byron
was sparingly conceded to us, and that of Shelley forbidden'.[4]
She was, however, taught Italian, French, and German, and her
horizons were greatly widened when her eldest brother Samuel
brought back from his travels in Europe some of the latest
literature: Lamartine, Balzac, Goethe, Herder, Richter, even
George Sand. She found that 'to one who had been brought up
after the strictest rules of New England Puritanism' these books
gave her a sense of intellectual excitement that was 'half
delightful, half alarming'.[5] Her father was shocked to find her
reading Goethe's *Faust*, which he had tried in translation and
pronounced 'a wicked book'.[6] Presumably his children were
careful to keep him away from George Sand.

It was a comfortable and privileged childhood in many ways,
but she was clearly frustrated by the atmosphere of her home. 'I
seemed to myself', she wrote, 'like a young damsel of olden
time, shut up within an enchanted castle. And I must say that
my dear father, with all his noble generosity and overweening
affection, sometimes appeared to me as my jailer.'[7] He died in
1839, when she was twenty, leaving her with this romantic

personal history. She might have stepped out of a novel by Henry James, or been the model for one of his rich heroines: the inexperienced girl, from an old military family, deeply affected by the inescapable Puritanism of her time and place, but fascinated by the new European thought.

Two years later, on a visit to Boston in 1841, she met Dr Samuel Gridley Howe, who was then teaching a blind and deaf-mute child, and who became the principal of the Institution for the Blind. Howe, who was eighteen years older than she was, had fought in the War of Greek Independence, and she delighted in the description of him as a hero. According to the *American National Biography*, the marriage was not always a happy one, perhaps because she was determinedly finding her own independence in Boston, both religiously and politically. She became a member of the Unitarian congregation under the radical Theodore Parker, who astonished Bostonians by praying to God, 'Father and Mother of us all',[8] and when Parker retired she continued to worship (in spite of her husband's uneasiness) at the Unitarian Chapel under James Freeman Clarke. Meanwhile she met those people who made Boston the centre for a time of the anti-slavery movement, William Lloyd Garrison, Charles Sumner (the senator for Massachusetts), and Wendell Phillips. These figures, and the successive Unitarian ministers, were radically different from the clergymen whom she had known in New York. She recalled one of those, the incumbent of a fashionable town church, saying at her father's dinner table: 'If I could get hold of one of those men who are trying to stir up the slaves of the South to cut their masters' throats, I would hang him to that lamp-post.'[9]

In Boston, everything was different. Garrison, who was editing *The Liberator*, and such figures as John Greenleaf Whittier, were writing indefatigably about the evils of slavery. Harriet Beecher Stowe's *Uncle Tom's Cabin*, published in 1852, was read with tears of emotion and anger. To Julia Ward Howe's house in South Boston came all kinds of people, including one who said that he wanted to be 'the saviour of the negro race', and whom she described as 'a Puritan of the Puritans, forceful, concentrated, and self-contained'.[10] His name was John Brown.

He was hanged on 2 December 1859 for his part in the attack on Harper's Ferry, a punishment that Victor Hugo said 'would thenceforth hallow the scaffold, even as the death of Christ had hallowed the cross'.[11] In such words, Brown was transformed from a Puritan extremist into a Christian martyr.

When the Civil War began, less than two years later, she and her husband followed the reports of the battles with an intense interest. She maintained that, with his experience of fighting in the Greek war, he was able to analyse the first account of such engagements quickly and accurately. But although he may have been a hero in 1822, he was too old to fight in this war. Her children were too young to do so. She knew that she was not one of those 'whose sons or husbands were fighting our great battle'.[12] She also knew that there were women who were working in the hospitals, or in administration, and that her family ties in Boston prevented her from doing the same. She was compelled, for these reasons, to be a spectator rather than a participant. But she wanted to be an informed spectator, and, in the autumn of 1861, she and her husband decided to see things for themselves. They set out for Washington, together with the governor of Massachusetts, John A. Andrew, and her minister, James Freeman Clarke. The time was not propitious. In July the first battle of Bull Run had ended in full retreat for the northern army. Lincoln was an anxious man throughout the autumn: when the party from Massachusetts had an audience with him, Clarke thought that the President's face bore an expression of 'hopeless honesty'.[13] Relations were strained between Lincoln and General George McLellan, who was steadily but very slowly rebuilding and training the Army of the Potomac; it was this army that was encamped around Washington. Thanks to the photographs that have survived from the war, we can see what the visitors saw: picket lines, tents, cooking-ranges, sentries, regiments drilling, the reading of orders, firing practice, sometimes just the standing about in groups as soldiers do. From time to time there were more formal occasions, which were intended to demonstrate the improved state of the army. One was the troop review on 20 November, attended by the

President and other high-ranking figures, to which the Massachusetts party was invited.

The review was meant to be a set-piece occasion to show the army in full marching order. But the Confederates, confident and resourceful after Bull Run, were only ten miles from Washington, and had other ideas: spoiling the party would be a propaganda coup, and would undermine morale in the Union army still further. The formality of the review was disturbed by a small attacking force, which had to be confronted and driven off. The remaining regiments were ordered back to their lines, marching off as quickly as possible. The spectators, apart from the presidential party, had to wait, and then had to travel back to Washington at a snail's pace.

Seldom can a traffic jam have had such a profound effect on a nation's identity. Howe described the scene herself:

> My dear minister was in the carriage with me, as were several other friends. To beguile the rather tedious drive, we sung from time to time snatches of the army songs so popular at that time, concluding, I think, with
>
> > 'John Brown's body lies a-mouldering in the ground;
> > His soul is marching on.'
>
> The soldiers seemed to like this, and answered back, 'Good for you!' Mr Clarke said, 'Mrs Howe, why do you not write some good words for that stirring tune?' I replied that I had often wished to do this, but had not as yet found in my mind any leading toward it.[14]

Clarke would have known that Howe was a poet: she had published two volumes of poetry, anonymously, during the previous decade (*Passion Flowers*, 1850; *Words for the Hour*, 1857). His suggestion was sensible and timely: its effect was almost instantaneous. She went to bed in Willard's Hotel that night, and slept well, but woke 'in the gray of the morning twilight':

and as I lay waiting for the dawn, the long lines of the desired poem began to twine themselves in my mind. Having thought out all the stanzas, I said to myself, 'I must get up and write these verses down, lest I fall asleep again and forget them.' So, with a sudden effort, I sprang out of bed, and found in the dimness an old stump of a pen which I remembered to have used the day before. I scrawled the verses almost without looking at the paper.[15]

Then she went back to bed and fell asleep again, 'Saying to myself, "I like this better than most things that I have written"'.[16] I think that the business of composition is very interesting: no doubt her mind had been somehow busy during the night, as Milton's was when he was writing *Paradise Lost*; but we notice other things. She wakens in the grey dawn, like a soldier, with the lines of the poem as her reveille. She knows, like a soldier, that it is her duty to get out of bed and write it down. So, with a sudden effort, against her own inclination to lie comfortably in the warm hotel bed, she springs out of it and writes. Now the 'old stump of a pen' becomes her most powerful weapon. It had been used for something unimportant the day before, but now it suddenly makes her war effort.

The poem was published on 14 January 1862 in the *New York Daily Tribune*, and then in the *Atlantic Monthly* for February 1862. In the second printing the final verse was omitted, at Howe's request. It began to be sung by Union soldiers, and to be called by them the 'Battle Hymn'. Chaplain McCabe, of the 122nd Ohio Volunteer Infantry, committed the hymn to memory, and taught it to those who (like himself) had been made prisoners of war, who sang it on hearing the news of Gettysburg. The manuscript, on Willard's Hotel notepaper, was kept by Howe and reproduced, like some battle-flag or precious war souvenir (the scrawl of the writing was like the dust or tatters on a flag), in *The Century Magazine* of 1887 and in Howe's *Reminiscences* of 1900.

It is not difficult to see why the poem formed itself in her mind so quickly and powerfully. Into its lines went so much of Howe's experience as a child and a woman, gathered up and given energy by the troop review that she had seen the previous day and the excitement of the visits to the Army of the Potomac in the weeks before. The formative instincts of her childhood are found in it: her knowledge of her ancestors and her pride in coming from a military family; the force of the Puritanism that she rebelled against but also admired in her father; the pattern of seeing her husband as a hero, yet determinedly resisting his patriarchal domination. What happened in the poem's writing was that she freed herself, at least temporarily, from father and husband. In her vision she moved beyond their reach, both in her imagination and also in creating something neither of them could have created. There was also the influence of the Boston anti-slavery movement and of Boston Unitarianism, with its high moral purpose; and its belief in righteousness and judgement. As Edmund Wilson has written, 'this vision of Judgment was the myth of the North'.[17]

We may take this vision of judgement also as a rebellion against those acquaintances of her father who wanted to see revolts in the south punished by hanging from lamp-posts, and against her father himself, the New York banker and non-soldier of the family, who loved her but who became her jailer and shut her up in an enchanted castle. With the word 'free' at the end of the penultimate verse, Howe fused her own need with that of the southern slaves; and the anti-slavery cause gave her an excuse to be as enthusiastic as she wanted to be in the cause of freedom, as liberal in her thinking as she liked. The occasion legitimized her own rebellion against father or husband: she had permission from her minister to break out from the imprisonment in the enchanted castle of her childhood; to disregard her husband's anxieties, or his restrictions on her independence, which were repeating the pattern in her later life.

The permission was granted, and joyfully received, because this was to be the moment at which oppression and slavery were to be swept away in the Civil War that was also the Day of Judgement. As Wilson put it, 'if we study the Civil War as a political or an economic phenomenon, we may fail to be aware of the apocalyptic aspect it wore for many defenders of the

Union'.[18] His comment points to the pervasive influence of the book of Revelation, of the visionary: 'And he that sat upon the throne said, Behold, I make all things new' (Revelation 21.5). That influence is clear in the last verse of Howe's poem (not reprinted after the poem's first appearance, and marked here with square brackets), echoing Revelation 22.20: 'Surely I come quickly. Amen. Even so, come, Lord Jesus.' That verse, at that historical time, was part of what might be called the deep structure of the war's grammar, the underlying ideological energy that lay beneath the troop movements, the training-camps and the picket lines. Wilson identifies it as the resurgence of 'the old fierceness, the old Scriptural assertiveness of the founders of the New England theocracy'.[19] Howe's moral purpose, and her instant poetic response to Clarke's suggestion, may indeed have come from this ancestral source just as surely as it came from Unitarianism or the Boston liberalism of William Lloyd Garrison.

In 1861, Howe was forty-three years old, in the prime of her mature life, but without a role, principally because she was a woman and a mother. Many other women found a purpose during the Civil War: Elizabeth Young, in *Disarming the Nation*, described the war as 'a concentrated moment of social flux, [which] catalysed and authorized multiple modes of civil disobedience for women'.[20] The war enabled them to become nurses, orderlies, or workers in the Sanitation Department. Howe was none of these, as she pointedly noted in her *Reminiscences*. Nor was she, like the March family in *Little Women*, one of those who waited anxiously at home while the father and husband was away. She had no prospect of being a war-mother, or a war-widow. Her response was to break out from the boundaries more spectacularly than any of the others by taking on the traditionally male role of the prophet. She crossed the gender line by assuming the patriarchal prerogative of vision and denunciation: 'Mine eyes have seen the glory of the coming of the Lord.' It is breathtaking in its confident assumption of the prophetic mantle. The very first word asserts her own right to the visionary power: '*Mine* eyes have seen the glory.'

The first verse is Julia Ward Howe's restatement of the opening of Isaiah 63, itself a majestic statement of God coming in righteousness, glorious in his apparel, great in his strength and mighty to save. The sublimity of the passage is well calculated to create awe and wonder, speaking as it does of vengeance, righteousness and salvation. The winepress is the process by which, laboriously but also violently, the winejuice is separated from the skins and stalks of the grapes: it is a symbol, found elsewhere in the Old Testament, of the judgement of Yahweh. Commentators, rather feebly, have found this passage hard to take: James D. Smart stands for a number of them when he says that 'the dramatic opening passage . . . has troubled many interpreters because of what has seemed to them to be its savagery', but he goes on to argue that 'neither for Second Isaiah nor for any other prophet could there be a day of salvation without a day of judgement'.[21] Julia Ward Howe was made of sterner stuff than the commentators: she does not go in for hand-wringing over the violence of the passage, but takes it over with enthusiasm.

The interpreters of Isaiah 63 operate on a scale between the mythological at one end and the historical at the other. This is not of great interest for the 'Battle Hymn', except to note that the historically based annotation tends curiously to emphasize the kind of experience that Howe had had the day before: an army coming to the rescue of Judah, having already taken vengeance on Edom and Bozrah, which were south of Jerusalem, and which had plundered Judah during its defenceless period following the Babylonian exile. It would be entirely possible, though I think implausible, to suggest that there was an elaborate connection in Howe's mind between the south (Edom and Richmond, Virginia), and the avenging army around Washington (or Judah). I mention it rather because it highlights the close connection in general terms between the perception of Yahweh as a mighty avenging figure, bloodstained and victorious, and Howe's chance to see the military might that was being prepared in the autumn of 1861. The Army of the Potomac could, in this apocalyptic ideology described by Edmund Wilson, become strangely fused with ancient myth: for example, one of the best commentators on this passage, Claus Westermann, describes the first phrases of Isaiah 63 as 'the sentry's cry' – Who is this that cometh? Who goes there?[22] The challenge of the guards around the picket lines is paralleled in the phrasing of Second Isaiah.

Perhaps for these reasons, the opening of Isaiah 63 was the passage that engaged Howe as 'the long lines . . . began to twine themselves in my mind'. The long lines are important; they carry the energy and movement further than one expects. 'Mine eyes have seen the glory' does not end the line, which continues on, and then on, further than one would expect: 'of the coming of the Lord' . There is not one adjectival phrase but two, the second identifying the comer as the Old Testament Yahweh, but also perhaps as the redeemer, Christ in majesty, 'mighty to save' (verse 1), so that 'the year of my redeemed is come' (verse 4). He is trampling out the vintage, the phrase coming from verse 3: 'I will tread them in mine anger, and trample them in my fury'; but these are the grapes of wrath, not the grapes that were the traditional symbol of Jesus Christ, the true vine, whose blood is tasted by us as the wine of the holy communion. The first two lines seem to hold out the possibility of the New Testament coming – 'Even so, come, Lord Jesus' – only to return to the Old Testament figure of the God who said 'Vengeance is mine', here equipped with the fateful lightning of his terrible swift sword.

The lines 'twined themselves' in her mind. The passage from Isaiah 63 was 'twined' with the tune she and her friends had sung that previous afternoon, with its heavy iambic beat, suddenly changing in the refrain to the trochaic 'Glory, glory'. As the best hymns do, this one blended words and music to make something other than the sum of its parts, more than words plus music: the two were fused to make a rhythmical, swinging line, allowing the words to be pushed along and yet giving space for the ideas of each line to grow. The tune began, it is believed, as a composition by a Philadelphia musician, William Steffe, for a company of firemen in Charleston, South Carolina. It was taken over and given new words for evangelical revivals: 'Say, brothers will you meet us/ On Canaan's happy shore?' It seems to have made the leap to John Brown's body because of the 2nd Battalion of Massachusetts Infantry, which had a sergeant called John Brown. In some camp entertainment in 1861, the evangelical hymn was given new words, partly no doubt for comic reasons, for it is said that John Brown was the butt of many jokes, such as, 'He has a lively gait for a corpse'. But it must have spread through the army as an anti-slavery song, in various versions, remembering the raid on Harper's Ferry and its consequences. One army song seems to have been 'We will hang Jeff Davis on a sour apple tree'. By the time Julia Ward Howe and her friends came to Washington, it was well enough known to be sung by them, presumably without a book, and applauded by the soldiers who were marching by.

Her use of it moves easily between the mythological and biblical sublimity of the first verse to the army camped around Washington in the second. The regiments are glimpsed, their tents pitched around the watch-fires in the damp November evenings, their lines illuminated by lamps, some bright, some dim. As soldiers read orders by the light of the lamps, so the poet reads God's sentence in the army itself: the army becomes a kind of exemplum itself, a text in which one can read the righteous sentence, 'sentence' here having the primary meaning of 'judgement'. And the reader, of course, is 'I', the prophet-poet: 'I have seen . . . I have read'. The reading goes on in the next verse: now the text is reread, as though it is a rich and complex emblem, capable of being no longer a righteous sentence but a fiery gospel. It is 'read', that is interpreted from the 'writing', which is 'writ in burnished rows of steel', presumably the highly polished bayonets of a trained army, whose discipline is indicated in its shining ranks of well-drilled soldiers.

What that gospel says is fiery indeed. It is the twenty-fifth chapter of St Matthew's Gospel, which contains the parable of the sheep and the goats. The occasion is the day of judgement, 'when the Son of man shall come in his glory, and all the holy angels with him'. Then he will receive those who have fed the hungry or taken in the stranger, or cared for the sick or visited the prisoners. Howe adds to this list: the grace of God will be given to those who 'deal with my contemners', with those who despise God and his laws. The balance of the line – 'As ye deal . . . so with you my grace shall deal' – takes us back in St Matthew's Gospel to chapter 7, verse 2: 'with what judgment ye judge, ye shall be judged'. The reward will come to those who act rightly, the grace of God to those who deal with the contemners.

The speaker here is Christ, speaking of himself in the third person, as he does in St Matthew's Gospel: 'When the Son of man shall come in his glory.' Now he is 'the hero born of woman', the incarnate Christ who will crush the serpent of the world's evil. This is a reference to Revelation 12.9, where 'the great dragon was cast out, that old serpent, called the Devil', and to Romans 16.20, where 'the God of peace shall bruise Satan under your feet shortly'. The army is an instrument not only of this final judgement but also of progress towards that day: 'God is marching on', his powerful campaign reiterated in the drilled repetition of the fourth line of each verse, each fourth line in step with the ones before, the verses marching on and on.

The trumpet of the fourth verse is blown by Christ himself, the hero. It is the traditional battle trumpet, the instrument used by Joshua and Gideon, yet also the signal for the final battle, and the trumpet that shall sound at the day of judgement. It may have come into her mind during the Washington days, when Howe would have heard the bands and bugles, but they were ordinary trumpets, whereas this is the transfiguring trumpet, even as the army itself is transfigured into this glorious instrument of God's campaigning will. As it sounds, we are reminded again, in a kind of parenthesis, that God 'is sifting out the hearts of men', that we choose between good and evil: the trumpet calls the advance, and the poet replies: 'O, be swift, my soul, to answer him; be jubilant, my feet!'

At this point she is no longer 'seeing' or 'reading', but responding and running: the trumpet calls, and she runs to answer, with jubilation. She becomes a recruit in the army of the Lord, even if she cannot become an actual recruit to the

Army of the Potomac. But that army has, in the course of the poem, become God's instrument, and she hastens to be a part of the marching regiments of the Lord. Edmund Wilson, however, sees that line, 'O be swift, my soul', as linked with the previous one: 'The Lord is apparently checking on those who do and those who do not enlist, so hurry up and join the Lord's army!'[23] This seems to be not only inappropriate in its tone, but also a misreading of the text: Howe is not recruiting here so much as entering the poem herself, as she volunteers for service. The moment frees her, allows her to forget her own circumstances, her gender, her family, her elderly husband. Like Keats when he is possessed by the nightingale, she is transported through the poem into a world in which visions are possible: in her excited imagination she becomes momentarily this jubilant warrior, her sex lost in the possibility of being a part of the great army whose camp fires she had seen in the previous days.

The key word here is 'transfigures':

> In the beauty of the lilies Christ was born across the sea,
> With a glory in his bosom that transfigures you and me.

The sudden switch to Christ, and the strange image of the lilies, are part of the process by which the poem moves on a journey, like the 'Ode to a Nightingale', from the circumstantial to the imaginative. The birth of Christ is located 'across the sea', away from all this military activity in Washington, and his birth is marked by lilies, the white flowers of innocence and the flowers of beauty, so beautiful that even Solomon in all his glory was not arrayed like one of these. The word 'glory' occurs in this verse, for the first time since the opening line of the poem, and it carries a magnificence that is both religious and military. The glimpses of the lilies and the Christ-child in glory are part of the vision in which the poet is herself radiant in her answer to the trumpet call that signals both the marching army and the Day of Judgement. But then, remembering Christ's death, she reaches for the parallel:

As he died to make men holy, let us die to make men free,
While God is marching on.

Christ's death was, like his birth, 'across the sea', and its purpose was to change humankind. But we will bring something like it to America. Now it is our time to change humankind, not universally but in the nation, in that republic whose battle hymn this is. The soldiers with their burnished rows of steel are engaged in an activity that may be deadly to themselves as well as to others, but in that activity they will, if they die, have died to make men free, even as Christ died to free humankind from the power of sin. And Howe, in her transfigured state, goes with them: 'let us die to make men free'. Let us live our lives in a campaign against wickedness, against slavery, against systems that degrade and humiliate our fellow human beings.

Howe's transfiguration from spectator to participant is complete, and it allows her to become a part of the great army that is marching on. It is this engagement that invites us to consider the relationship of the poem to Christian spirituality. At first sight, it does not seem to have much to contribute to our understanding of spirituality: it is a poem about armies, soldiers, watch-fires, circling camps. Spirituality is traditionally thought of as striving towards a union with the divine, often through prayer and self-denial, and through the first half of the Christian era it was often associated with austerity or the practice of monasticism. But, as *The Oxford Companion to Christian Thought* has put it, 'the diversities of Christian spirituality are much influenced by the various cultures of Christian history',[24] from the ethics of the early Christians, to the abandoning of the world by the Desert Fathers, to monasticism and (after the Reformation) to a spirituality described by Max Weber as 'intra-mundane', this-worldly. 'Spirituality', according to the *Companion*, 'is essentially life in the Holy Spirit, the life and love of God himself, released by the death and glorification of Jesus Christ. Grounded in a sense of incarnation, it both transcends and involves the material and the physical'.[25]

This is a basic definition only, but it is helpful when considering the Battle Hymn of the Republic. In that hymn, Howe perceives, through the power of her prophetic and poetic imagination, the glory of the coming of the Lord. She acknowledges the glorification of Jesus Christ, and his death – 'as he died to make men holy' – and the poem is certainly ' grounded in a sense of incarnation': Christ is 'born across the sea' and it is his glory that transfigures us, just as it begins and ends the hymn. In that process, the poem both transcends and involves the material and physical, because it was grounded in the troop review of 20 November 1861, still fresh in Howe's mind as she awoke the following morning; and yet it was also expressive of a whole transfiguring spirituality that saw in those military manoeuvres a gospel of righteousness and freedom. And if the incarnate Christ was born 'across the sea', this poem brings his presence to America.

The hymn also reflects 'the diversities of Christian spirituality' in their relationship with history. If we measure the diversities of spirituality on a scale with the ascetics at one end and the participants in the world of action at the other, then Howe's hymn could be perceived as being at the extreme end of the *vita activa* part of the spectrum. As a Unitarian, she would naturally be drawn to the life of daily morality and practical goodness. But to see it as an expression of an ethical or moral position would be to oversimplify it, and there are other elements in it that need to be considered.

Howe would have been drawn, for example, to that part of Christian spirituality that saw the necessity for fighting against wickedness. The principal texts for this are the Old Testament stories of Joshua, Gideon and David, but also St Paul's description of the armour of God in Ephesians 6. This is the subject of a hymn such as Charles Wesley's 'Soldiers of Christ, arise'. In the nineteenth century, however, a new note appears in hymnody: whereas Wesley was basically using the whole armour of God as defence, Reginald Heber writes, 'The Son of God goes forth to war'. Christ goes out now to conquer, which is one reason why the mission field was so important in those years. On that 'field' the battle against heathenism was fought, and soldier hymns abounded in the nineteenth century, from 'Onward, Christian soldiers' to 'For all the saints who from their labours rest'. Missionaries, the shock troops of the Christian religion, died in their hundreds of disease and fatigue, heroic martyrs for the faith.

Martyrdom led, and still leads, to a union with Christ. We sing in the *Te Deum* of 'the noble army of martyrs'. The idea has been taken over for dead soldiers and recorded on war memorials as 'the supreme sacrifice', the laying down of one's life for a cause. In the Battle Hymn of the Republic it is the climactic moment of the transfiguration: 'As he died to make men holy, let us die to make men free.' In dying, the soldiers become transfigured, even as Wilfred Owen, in a moment of imaginative empathy, saw them as Christ-figures, drilling by numbers. So the crosses in the war-memorial cemeteries in France and Flanders and Burma and elsewhere have a sword embedded in the cross as a potent symbol of the union of the soldier's and the Christian's life. Soldiers become martyrs, as Julia Ward Howe invites them to do, in the cause of freedom.[26]

But Christian spirituality is such a complex phenomenon that we should not limit it to martyrdom, or to self-sacrifice. I can approach it best, and most briefly in the time that I have, by taking one passage from a single writer for use in this context. I choose Schleiermacher because he is a representative of that Romantic-period theology that leads directly into the thought of the nineteenth century, and to those Coleridge-inspired transcendentalists in Boston who taught Julia Ward Howe during the 1840s and 1850s. In *The Christian Faith*, in the second edition of 1830, there is a section in the ' Second Part of the System of Doctrine' that is concerned with 'The Communication of the Holy Spirit': *The Holy Spirit is the union of the Divine Essence with human nature in the form of the common Spirit animating the life in common of believers.* In it he writes:

> Now if the Holy Spirit is an effective spiritual power in the souls of believers, we must either represent Him as bound up with their human nature, or we shall have to surrender the unity of their being, if on the one hand they are such that in

them human nature shows itself in operation, and on the other, such that in them the Holy Spirit is acting in separation from human nature. To adopt such a view would produce so entire a dualism within human life that it could never be maintained.[27]

The leading of the Holy Spirit is never other than a divine incitement to realize the standard of what Christ, in virtue of the being of God in Him, humanly was and did.[28]

I find these extracts useful because they can be related to Howe's poem, which is clearly representing God and the Holy Spirit as 'bound up' with our human nature. In the hymn, she perceives, through the poetic spirit of her imagination, the glory of the coming of the Lord. She acknowledges the glorification of Jesus Christ, and his death – 'as he died to make men holy' – and the poem is certainly grounded in the sense of incarnation, 'of what Christ, in virtue of the being of God in Him, humanly was and did': in the hymn, Christ is 'born across the sea', and it is his glory that transfigures us, just the form and shape of the hymn are in part determined by its beginning and ending, in which that glory is expressed. In that process, the hymn rejects what Schleiermacher would call the 'dualism within human life'. It asserts what Schleiermacher affirms elsewhere in this section, that 'the Holy Spirit is not something that, although divine, is not united with the human nature, but only somehow influences it from without'.[29] Howe's hymn, as I have suggested, similarly both transcends and involves the material and physical.

So when I said that Howe's hymn was at one end of the spectrum of spirituality that runs from world-abandonment at one end to 'intra-mundane' conduct at the other, I was oversimplifying to the extent that Howe's hymn also shows the way in which spirituality involves freedom, transformation, a transcending of the physical as well as an involvement in the physical. What happens in the hymn is that her poetic imagination allows both transcendence and involvement, transfiguration and engagement with the world. And finally, it relates her experience to what Schleiermacher called 'the life in common of believers', or 'the common spirit', in which she, as a woman, a wife and mother, sees the whole great untidy army and is united with its soldiers, finding herself part of its common life in her transfigured mode. Here is Schleiermacher again:

> The divine activity constituting the new life in the individual is common spirit for this additional reason, that it is in each without regard to personal peculiarities, provided only he belongs to the fellowship through the influence of which his regeneration was conditioned, and out of which, by preaching in the widest sense of the word, this new life was transmitted to him, exactly as it took shape in the disciples through the power of the self-communicating life of Christ.[30]

The Battle Hymn of the Republic is, significantly, in part about the common life. It began in a moment that obliterated differences and transcended identities; and its continued life has been so lusty and energetic because it celebrates the Holy Spirit in the world, and especially in the life in common of a nation. It was sung at the funeral service for Abraham Lincoln in 1865, and in the service at St Paul's Cathedral in 1951 to commemorate the American soldiers who died in the Second World War; it was sung at the memorial service for Sir Winston Churchill in 1965, and at that for Robert F. Kennedy in 1968. Four thousand people sang it at Julia Ward Howe's own funeral in 1910. It must have been sung, over and over again, at great occasions, accumulating to itself the resonance that comes from such repetition at time of great emotion, often national grief and emotion, shared in common by people who would normally lead separate lives. Its phrases have become, as I said at starting, part of the American experience, seeds for other writers, titles for their books: John Steinbeck's *The Grapes of Wrath*; two volumes of Bruce Catton's *Centennial History of the Civil War*, (*Terrible Swift Sword* and *Never Call Retreat*); and more recently, *In the Beauty of the Lilies*, John Updike's story of an American family in the twentieth century. Steinbeck was thrilled with *The Grapes of Wrath* for a title:

I like it because it is a march and this book is a kind of march – because it is in our own revolutionary tradition and because in reference to this book it has a large meaning. And I like it because people know the Battle Hymn who don't know the Star Spangled Banner.[31]

Updike's novel begins, perhaps intentionally, in 1910, the year of Howe's death, with a minister losing his faith; it ends in 1990 with the minister's great-grandson making a terrible rediscovery of religion in a mad and dangerous sect. Updike's brilliant quotation of a verse from the Battle Hymn of the Republic as an epigraph becomes a powerful, almost radiant, reminder of an older and stabler world, of a morality and a belief that, it sometimes seems, no longer command a consensus. There may be individual goodness, and the hymn may still be sung, but Updike's message is bleaker than Steinbeck's, and the hymn is there to show what, on the whole, no longer resonates (that, of course, is not a criticism of the hymn, but a criticism of American society between 1910 and 1990). Nevertheless, it remains an ideal, an aspiration, a hymn still sung at Commencement, a part of Schleiermacher's 'common life': a hope that exists in spite of everything, a rebellion (one might say, bringing Camus in to the argument) against the pointlessness and superficiality that Updike describes so effectively. These are a testimony to the extraordinary power of a hymn that was written to change the words of a song, but which transcended that aim, just as it allowed the author to see herself, for a moment on a grey November morning in a hotel bedroom, as freed, exalted and transfigured. And then she went back to bed, and got on with the rest of her life.

Notes

1 Julia Ward Howe, *Reminiscences, 1819–1899* (Boston and New York, Houghton, Mifflin & Co., 1900), p. 4. (Hereafter *Reminiscences*).

2 *Reminiscences*, p. 18.

3 *Reminiscences*, p. 22.

4 *Reminiscences*, p. 58.

5 *Reminiscences*, p. 59.

6 *Reminiscences*, p. 59.

7 *Reminiscences*, p. 49.

8 *Reminiscences*, p. 166.

9 *Reminiscences*, p. 61.

10 *Reminiscences*, p. 254.

11 *Reminiscences*, p. 256.

12 *Reminiscences*, p. 273.

13 *Reminiscences*, p. 272.

14 *Reminiscences*, pp. 274–5.

15 *Reminiscences*, p. 275.

16 *Reminiscences*, p. 275.

17 Edmund Wilson, *Patriotic Gore* (London, André Deutsch, 1962), p. 91.

18 Edmund Wilson, *Patriotic Gore*, p. 91.

19 Edmund Wilson, *Patriotic Gore*, p. 91.

20 Elizabeth Young, *Disarming the Nation* (Chicago and London, University of Chicago Press, 1998), p. 14.

21 James D. Smart, *History and Theology in Second Isaiah* (Philadelphia, PA, The Westminster Press, 1965), p. 266.

22 Claus Westermann, *Isaiah 40–66* (London: SCM Press, 1966), p. 381.

23 Wilson, *Patriotic Gore*, p. 95.

24 Adrian Hastings (ed.), *The Oxford Companion to Christian Thought* (Oxford, Oxford University Press, 2000), p. 685.

25 Hastings (ed.), *Companion*, p. 685.

26 I am not sure how easy it is to read the Battle Hymn of the Republic, with its call to martyrdom, after the tragic events of 11 September 2001. We are confronted there with the prospect of martyrdom as violent, and as involving the death of others. This is, of course, present in any war situation, and is latent in Howe's poem, but she avoids it: the soldiers of the Union army, who were being trained to kill Confederates, are exhorted to 'die to make men free' not to 'kill to make men free'.

27 Friedrich Schleiermacher, *The Christian Faith*, tr. and ed. H. R. Mackintosh and J. S. Stewart (Edinburgh, T. & T. Clark, 1928), p. 572.

28 Schleiermacher, *Christian Faith*, p. 576.
29 Schleiermacher, *Christian Faith*, p. 571.
30 Schleiermacher, *Christian Faith*, p. 574.
31 Elaine Steinbeck and Robert Wallsten (eds), *Steinbeck. A Life in Letters* (London, Heinemann, 1975), p. 171.

INDEX

Alcuin 38–9; comments on Lord's Prayer 42–52 *passim*
Alfred the Great 38
Allison, Dale 90
Ambrose, St 63
American Civil War 125–6, 128–9
Amvrosy of Optino 28 n.41
Angelus 75, 84–5
Anomoeans 13
Anselm 78
Antony, St (Desert Father) 12
apocalyptic 128–9, 130
Apollo (Desert Father) 10, 11–12
apophatic prayer 13–14, 23–4
Apostles' Creed 56–74; Bede on 36
arrow prayers 11, 19
Augustine, St 56–7, 65, 90–2, 106

Baker, Frank 110
Baker, Henry Williams 105
Baldwin of Ford 77, 78
Balthasar, Hans Urs von 62, 67, 70, 72
baptism 6, 68; liturgy 63
Barsanuphius, St 2
Basil the Great, St 13
Battle Hymn of the Republic 121–42
Beatitudes 88–102
Bede 33–9; comments on Lord's Prayer 40–9 *passim*
Bernardino of Siena 84

Bethge, Eberhard 99
Bonhoeffer, Dietrich 98–100
Bossuet, J. B. 89–90
Brown, John 124–5, 132

Cabasilas, Nicholas 100
canon ix
Cappadocian Fathers 13
Cassian, John 10–11, 32–3; comments on Lord's Prayer 40–50 *passim*
catechesis 64–5
Charles V (Emperor) 119
Christ *see* Jesus
Christian life xi
Civil War (American) 125–6, 128–9
Clarke, James Freeman 125, 126
community of the Church 70–2, 100
confessions of faith 63–4
credal prayer 58–63
Creed, Apostles' 56–74; Bede on 36
creeds, early development 63–4
Cyprian, St 65

Dante Alighieri 94–6
David (King) 104
Desert Fathers 9–14, 135
Diadochus, St 15–25
disagreement among Christians xii

doctrine: and the creeds 60–1;
 and spiritual literature ix–x

Easter 114–17
Egyptian monasticism 8–13
Elias (Desert Father) 11
eternal life 119
Eunomius 13
Eusebius of Caesarea 89
Evagrius of Pontus 4, 13, 14, 20,
 23

Faustus of Rietz 74 n.26
fellowship of the Church 70–2,
 100
forgiveness 47–9
Fortunatus, Venantius 76

Garrison, William Lloyd 124
Gillet, Lev 28 n.41
Gogol, Nikolai 100–1
Gregory I (Pope) 77–8
Gregory of Nyssa 89, 92–3
Gregory Palamas, St 24
Gregory of Sinai 26 n.7
grief for sin 2, 11–12, 14, 16

Hail Mary 75–87
Hausherr, Irénée 12, 28 n.41
heaven 114, 115, 118
Heber, Reginald 136
Herbert, George 105, 107
Hermas 3
hesychasm 3–4, 13–14
Hesychius of Sinai, St 12–13
Hippolytus 63
Holy Spirit, gifts of 91
Howe, Julia Ward 122–32, 139
Howe, Samuel Gridley 124
hymn-singing 109–20

intellect 20–1
Isaac (Desert Father) 33
Isaac the Syrian, St 22

Jesus: death and resurrection 48,
 71, 114–17, 135, 138; humanity
 76; name 77–8 (see also Name
 of Jesus); teaching on prayer
 30; as victor 136
Jesus prayer 1–29
John Climacus, St 3
John of Gaza, St 2
judgement day 132–3

Kancheli, Guy 106
Kelly, J. N. D. 63
King, Charles 123
kingdom of God 43–4
koinonia (community of the
 Church) 70–2
Kucharek, Casimir 100

language, and spiritual literature
 xii
liturgical prayer 4, 59–62, 67;
 Alcuin on 38–9; see also Office
 of Our Lady
loneliness 67, 69–71
Lord's Prayer 30–55
Lubac, Henri de 61, 66
Lucius (Desert Father) 10, 11–12
Luther, Martin 73–4 n.18, 96–8

Macarian Homilies 15
Macarius of Egypt 10
Magonet, Jonathan 105
Manning, Bernard 111
Maranatha 3
Mark the Monk, St 18
Martineau, James 111
martyrdom 137

Mary 69; devotion to 75–6, 78–83
Mauriac, François 93
meekness 97–8
mercy, prayer for 3, 7–8, 10, 11–12
Meredith, Anthony 93
monks, Egyptian 8–13
monologic prayer 9–11
Moravians 109, 110
Moses de Leon (Rabbi) 107
mourning: in the Beatitudes 97; for sin 2, 11–12, 14, 16
mysteries of the rosary 82–3

Name of God 4–8, 42–3
Name of Jesus 3, 6–7, 11, 15–16, 18; baptism in 6; prayer in 6
naming 4–5
Nilus of Ancyra 27–8 n. 38

Office of Our Lady 79–82, 85
Origen 31–2, 88; comments on Lord's Prayer 43, 47, 50, 51
Our Father 30–55

Parker, Theodore 124
penitence 2, 11–12, 14, 16
personhood, levels of 21–5
Philemon (Desert Father) 1–2
Pius V (Pope) 84
prayer: apophatic 13–14, 23–4; credal 58–63; defined by Evagrius 20; in Jesus' name 6; monologic 9–11; in Origen's teaching 31–2; repetition 1, 3, 11, 16–19, 58, 82; in Teresa of Avila 39; without ceasing 1, 9; see also liturgical prayer; Lord's Prayer
Psalm 23 103–8
Psalms 1–2, 4, 9

pure prayer 3, 14, 23
purgatory 94–6

Rahner, Karl 62
Rattenbury, Ernest 112
rendering of the Creed 72 n.3
repetition of prayers 1, 3, 11, 16–19, 58, 82
rosary 24–5, 75, 82–4
Rufinus 63

sabbath 107
Sayers, Dorothy L. 94
Schillebeeckx, Edward 64
Schleiermacher, Friedrich 137–9
Serapion (Desert Father) 23
Sermon on the Mount 88, 90, 91
Shepherd of Hermas 3
Simplicianus 57
sinner, prayer of the 2, 8
Sisoes (Desert Father) 11, 12
slavery 124
Smart, James D. 130
spirituality 135–7
spiritual literature ix–xii
Steffe, William 131
Steinbeck, John 139–40
stillness 3–4, 13–14, 110
symbol of faith 65–6, 68

temptation 49–50
Teresa of Avila 39–40; comments on Lord's Prayer 41, 42, 43, 50
Tertullian 63
Theophan the Recluse 7, 9–10
Titian 119
Tolstoy, Leo 53
transfiguration 24, 134, 135, 136, 137

Trinity 68
Tugwell, Simon 89
Typika 100

Unitarianism 124, 128
Updike, John 139–40
Urban II (Pope) 80
Urban IV (Pope) 77

Velichkovsky, Paissy, St 8, 22
Victorinus, Marius 56–7, 65

Way of a Pilgrim, The 17
Weber, Max 135
Wesley, Charles 109–20, 136
Wesley, John 109, 110, 112, 118
Wilson, Edmund 134